D0188184

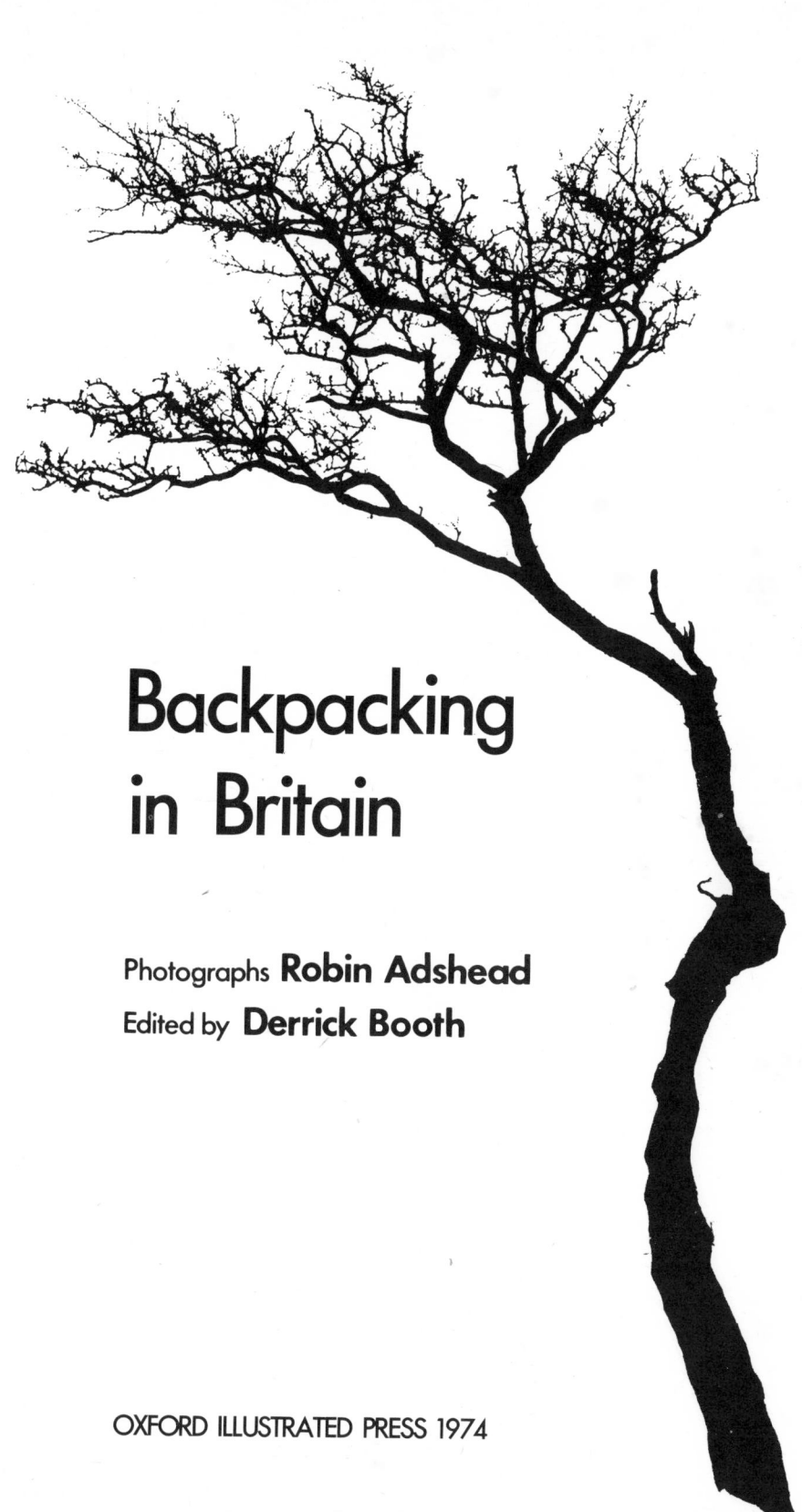

Backpacking in Britain

Photographs **Robin Adshead**
Edited by **Derrick Booth**

OXFORD ILLUSTRATED PRESS 1974

For Sally, Darrell and Corrin,
who make coming home so worthwhile.

This book is written in the hope that its
readers will derive as much pleasure from
backpacking as I do.

Many people have helped me to produce
Backpacking in Britain, either by allowing
themselves or their equipment to be photo-
graphed, or by giving advice, encouragement
and practical assistance. I am indebted to
John Adye, Chris Allen, Philip Green, Eric
Gurney, Jim Hayes, Peter Hutchinson, Tony
Lack, Peter Lumley, Tony Mayes, Dennis Noble,
Noble, Mike Parsons, George Raven and Jim
White for giving me the benefit of their time
and experience. John Hillaby has been kind
enough to pause from his famous travels to
write the foreword, and a better backpacking
friend than Derrick Booth I could not find. I
am grateful to them all.

Printed in Great Britain

ISBN 0 902280 21 X

© 1974 Robin Adshead and Oxford Illustrated Press

Oxford Illustrated Press · Shelley Close · Risinghurst · Oxford

Foreword by John Hillaby

President of the Backpackers' Club

Only the other day, as I rambled down the Ridgeway with a theme from Prokofiev running through my head, I thought how much there is in common between walking and music. The sense of elevation, the rhythm, the infinite variety of moods. It's all there. By music I don't mean only the rumpitty-tumitty-tum of martial brass. Think of the light-hearted classical tunes you know. Think of the bouncey bass notes of the great jazz men. March or walk, amble or ramble purposefully, and you can fit your stride to the greatest rhythms on earth. And when to this you add the changing panorama of landscapes, sky vistas and cloud patterns, the marvel is that people still ask what it is we get out of walking. The difficulty lies in communicating sheer pleasure to the unconverted. What can you tell them? It's useful, sometimes, to remember what Louis Armstrong once said.

Years ago, when that prince of horn players went back to his native New Orleans to give a concert, he said that before the show he mooched round and round the town "just to get the feel of the place." And then he went up to City Hall and played as he had never played before. The crowds were with him all the way. Encore followed encore. And when it was all over he leaned back, exhausted and answered questions from the press and television boys. Straight questions. Straight answers, especi-ally one that effectively put an end to the interview.

"Satchmo," said a man from AP. "Tell us. What is it *you* get outa jazz?" With sweat still pouring down that happily wrinkled face, Louis the Great looked up surprised. He sighed, deeply. He leaned forward and with theatrical deliberation said: "Man! If you gotta ask a question like that you'll *nevah* get to know."

It's much the same with walking. Much of the wonder and beauty of the world is not only within our grasp but there to be seen and felt, under our feet. But a word of caution to those who think they can immediately cast off the grey disease of conformity by striding out into clean air. Whilst anybody with a serviceable pair of legs can take a short breather, the backpacker has quite a lot to learn. The keynotes in C are Competence, Comfort and Confidence. The backpacker must cultivate a sense of indestructability. A fragment of grit under a sock, an ill-tied boot or shoe or a badly fitting pack can lay a day in ruins as effectively as the thorough soaking-through of the unprepared. What, for instance, is the most you can heft, pleasureably? Or the least without feeling bereft of simple comforts. It's questions of this kind that Robin Adshead sets out to answer, simply.

The rest is up to you. To quote Louis Armstrong once again: "Life is like a horn. You can only get out of it what you put in."

A few words from Robin Adshead

Backpacking possesses an instant appeal to some people. Possibly they have gone camping at one time or another, so that they are already over their possible nervousness of living out of doors. Such people need only bringing up to date on the latest space-age backpacking equipment. Others with no camping experience at all could be responding to an innate urge to slow down for a while, to do something out of their ordinary pattern or to take some exercise outside an ordered routine.

This book is intended to help the beginner backpacker through the equipment jungle and then to motivate him or her into getting out and using the gear that has been bought. It is hoped that it will help the novice from making too many mistakes in the first purchases. So many backpackers are the possessors of two complete sets of equipment, one of which is now all wrong for their present way of hiking.

The photographs in this book show some of the finest backpacking gear available in this country. At the back of the book are layouts of suggested kit for winter and summer packing in all conditions. It must be stressed here that not everything shown is absolutely necessary for every trip either for the experienced hiker or for the tyro going onto the trail for the first time. Indeed, a great deal of enjoyment can be had in good weather by merely taking a blanket and a plastic sheet for warmth and shelter, and a bag to hold some cold food and a bottle of water. With such light loads, any form of footwear will be adequate, and the beginner will be building up experience.

Anyone intending to take a serious interest in backpacking will sooner or later find that his comfort and safety will be better catered for if some of the precepts in this book are taken as a starting line. For those without large sums of loose cash, it is advisable to start slowly, buying nothing until you have looked at a lot of different equipment, preferably talking to some other people with practical experience of its use. Such advice is freely given in the better shops which sell backpacking gear, where the staff are mostly keen walkers themselves. The other source of information lies in the catalogues produced by the makers of backpacking paraphernalia, although only experience will tell you which one to believe.

The next question will be where to go for the first trip. Start close to home, with the option of coming back if the weather looks as if it will ruin the trip. Until you have more properly designed gear, you will not enjoy bad weather, and will be discouraged from going out again. You will probably find that the first hike will leave you feeling exhilarated with the sense of freedom and exercise, while lack of a piece of equipment leaves you frustrated and determined to fill the gap as soon as possible. Whatever you do at the beginning, make sure that you get a good night's rest, as nothing will discourage you more than a cold, sleepless night when you begin.

Too much damage has been done to our countryside by people who do not care what they do to it, and who think that such damage will repair itself overnight. Backpackers should approach the country in a totally different frame of mind, setting out purposefully to ensure that the enjoyment they feel when walking on our hills may be equally enjoyed by our children. Only by being aware and responsible countrygoers can backpackers make certain that their passing presence is welcomed by landowners and the authorities. The guide lines to behaviour in the country are well laid down in the Country Code, which should be used as a minimal starting point by backpackers, beginner and expert alike.

Backpacking is a very personal thing. There is such freedom of choice as to where to go, what to see, whether to go on or stop. Once in the chosen area there are no buses to catch or cars to park. Eat when you are hungry, stop when you are tired. No one can really tell you how to go, or what to take with you to conform with your own comfort level. You must find this out for yourself, as the experts have done. What suits me may not suit you, but you have to begin somewhere. This book tries to show you where to begin.

...and from Derrick Booth

A counter movement is already swimming against the great current of affluence. The young have already rebelled. The middle-aged take flabby bodies to saunas, gymnasia and participation field sports. The popular mountains attract car-borne adventurers in ever increasing numbers. The swimming pools are being filled just as fast as they can be built.

But there is a timelessness about walking. Feet have been the principle means of locomotion since man stood upright. They allowed him to migrate long before he tamed the horse. They still form a vital link between the various means of accelerated travel.

This book is about feet and the pleasures they can bring for those willing to use them with an intensity which was normal only half a century ago. Of course affluence has crept in to walking. Good boots are now well within the purchasing power of the masses. Affluence has made leisure activities a lot easier, but it has added a strata of stress which often negates the value of the leisure. The jetplane, the motorcar, the high-speed motor yacht, the packaged deal have all enriched our off-time activities, but have they made life fuller or only fulsome?

Being wide-ranging does not necessarily provide more time to consider detail. Air conditioned comfort may stabilise the seasons but it only serves to blur the natural divisions in the animal cycle of rising activity, maturity and subsidence; spring, summer, autumn and winter.

Affluence is also relative. Being better off financially does not necessarily secure a better state of mind. Often it brings quite the reverse and breeds materialism which is likely to satiate the pleasures of ownership much more rapidly.

Finely made packs drawing on space-age materials can be bought for less than a meal for four in a three star restaurant. Superb tents, sleeping bags, and clothing can be obtained for less than the cost of a long weekend in Paris in the spring.

When all these things are put together in a carefully considered matrix and directed towards improving the range of a pedestrian without recourse to a hotel or lodging, then a whole new way of leisure emerges. It is called backpacking.

Then the wonderful treasury of the British countryside lies under the sole of a boot, very often with no other human within sight or hailing distance. No manicured and amplified voice can announce that a flight to some tourist trap where the sun is supposed to shine has been delayed by fog, strike or accident. Only the wind calls as it combs through the hair and massages the carelines from the brow. Only the lark rises or the curlew trills . . .

Quite unashamedly, this book is a sales brochure for unknown Britain which beckons the man or woman who is willing to use muscle and mind to reach an objective. It sets out to demonstrate that the depth of one's pocket is not the criterion by which happiness can be achieved. Inflation cannot diminish the utter pleasure of seeing the unbelievable richness of Britain that has managed to escape the developer and the road builder. Nor can it detract from the even greater pleasure of falling happily asleep for a full eight hours after becoming physically tired by personal endeavour.

Britain contains ideal country for backpacking. Here's how to go about it.

Conditions of urban life cause frustration and stress in urban man and his family. Backpacking offers at least a temporary haven from such tension.

Backpacking in Britain

At its lowest level, backpacking is an exquisite form of masochism. There is no upper limit to the equally exquisite pleasure that can be derived from it.

Definitions are notoriously difficult, for backpacking can be all things to all people. For those who need such things however, a rough and ready definition is that backpacking is a way of enabling the hiker to wander where he will, dependent only upon a life support system carried on his back.

Backpacking is not a sport. Sport suggests competition, and backpacking is non-competitive. Some backpacking techniques are used in mountain orienteering races, but mountain racing is hardly what the genuine backpacker has in mind. A backpacker goes to the hills to exercise body and soul at strictly his own rate.

Backpacking is more a way of life than a tangible attainment. Your backpacker is essentially a romantic with a bee in his bonnet about his own ecological place in the order of the world. He shuns the sybaritic pleasures of industrial man at leisure and seeks the simpler, more esoteric pleasure of moving in a tiny part of a landscape. At the same time, he is by no means a Spartan; a romantic, yes, but a fool, never.

In the pages that follow, there should be enough inducement, through pictures and words, to introduce industrial man, his wife and children, to backpacking in our own magnificent country. Here is an invitation to discover what lies beyond the lane end and the car park by using feet that were evolved essentially for walking. If there is no inducement, at least there should be understanding, and above all, a practical demonstration of what it takes to live comfortably very close to the ground when others retire to their vulnerable homes believing that they have the better deal in life.

If you are not lame, weak of heart or totally afflicted in some way, the outdoors beckons you to a more active life. It urges you to cast off the cloaking concrete and go back to the green places of our island. Each year more concrete creeps insidiously over Britain; a new town here, and a motorway there. Soon the very access to the countryside will be regulated so that a small parcel of grossly devalued 'recreation area' is available for a fee, but none other. This hideous thought is not so far-fetched. It is happening now. The lifetime of a mature man living today may well be the last that allows almost unrestricted access to the beautiful, varied and satisfying land we call our country.

Backpacking is a means of seeing this threatened asset. Backpacking might well invest zeal into thousands who have the power to alter the inexorable tendency towards the nightmare of 'beautiful Britain' seen only from the steamy window of a coach which cannot deviate from a licensed route.

Why do it? Everyone reacts differently to this question. For some people it is purely physical. They hike vigorously to maintain a standard of health which is otherwise threatened in a factory, towering office block, smog-filled city street or claustrophobic tenement building.

There are others who suffer from extreme tension induced by industrialised living. It is possible to cast off this pressure, that of survival in an urban environment, by occasionally facing challenges not posed by people but by weather and terrain.

Yet another group, lonely in everyday life — introverted and even afraid to seek friendships — seek the loosely formed and soon ended relationships which can be discovered on the trail, the 'wandervogel' syndrome which blossomed in Europe in the 1930s. These people find a freer opportunity in backpacking than in other more regimented and proscribed recreations.

Then there is the astringent of fear — not hysteria but a whiff of fear which arises in all humans when they face entirely unknown situations for which they are unprepared. This astringency cleanses the soul and teaches by experience an entirely new level of confidence. The magnitude of the fear can range from a loose bull in a wide field that has to be traversed, to being caught in high places in a severe electrical storm (one of the most frightening things humans can face in the wild).

The backpacker whose senses are not aroused by little unfamiliar noises in the night, the ear-deadening blanket of soft falling snow, the strange symptoms

of hypothermia, would seem to be a person of limited imagination and foresight. Lack of reaction to such things could well lead to disaster, and such a person would be better off packing with a more perceptive companion.

Recognition of a problem is the first major step to its solution. The backpacker who recognises the primitive instinct of fear, and who can apply coolly an orderly mind to deduce the cause and bring effective relief stands a far greater chance of survival than one who goes blindly on in a marginal situation.

Despite affluence, the motor car and soft living, there are many for whom the budget will accommodate only a week or two at the seaside with the family, with nothing over to cover the other days of leisure. For this group, backpacking offers much reward for relatively little expenditure. Unlike so many organised activities where a man's equipment reflects the state of his purse, backpacking is a classless recreation which draws no sniffing from the better-off when a poor but enthusiastic newcomer strides down the footpath ahead. Some of the scruffiest backpackers are those with the deepest pockets.

Nor does one have to join an expensive club to make the grade. There is a Backpackers' Club, but it is for unclubbables, mavericks who otherwise would have no status when officialdom enquires.

Backpacking embraces all who wish to walk for more than one day without retiring to a fixed dwelling. Many pack alone. Others walk in small groups. Whole families don their boots and packs to idle through the landscape. All are motivated by a primitive urge.

This primeval motive has much to do with the basic impulse to go backpacking. Man's prime needs, food, shelter and companionship can be found in unsophisticated form when practising backpacking. The open fire draws most romantics and is the most universal sales promotion for outdoor life. Add a tent, a lone pine, a snow-capped mountain, a clear stream, the smell of resin, fresh coffee and the sound of larks and you have the picture-postcard sales brochure for backpacking . . .

The wide variety of equipment in a good backpacking shop will initially confuse the beginner.

Buying from a specialist shop will ensure that the backpacker does not emerge looking like this.

The first visit to a backpacking shop can be bewildering. You will greatly reduce your area of choice by telling the assistant that your interest is backpacking, not mountaineering or climbing. Then compare the very best in each section with the cheaper ranges, to note the difference in quality that more money buys.

It all starts with feet. Feet are the backpacker's vehicle once he forsakes his car. On those feet, softened by good living, must come an extra load and a pounding from an uneven trail over a distance between night stops.

Nothing will ever go right if feet are not properly cared for, conditioned and clad with the proper equipment. Foot disorders abound. Neglect which can be tolerated on a daily basis, which puts no more demand on feet than walking from home to car, car to office and return, is suicidal when the same feet are pitchforked into clay trails rising at a gradient of one in three.

If you have neglected your feet and yet aspire to backpacking, the most prudent thing to do is make an appointment with a chiropodist and get them examined and cared for. Ordinary feet — the soft ones, and the naturally hard and dry — can be coaxed into trim at home without recourse to professional help.

Nails must be trimmed square and shortish. Sore spots, hardskin corns and bunions must be attended to. Walking barefoot around the house at all times helps enormously. Bathing with surgical spirit works for some people and not for others, for there is really no substitute for walking properly clad.

That is why backpackers go for boots. The boot takes the punishment and not the foot — at least it does when boot and foot are properly matched. An improperly fitted boot is foolishly painful.

The space between the inside and the boot and the foot is filled with best wool. Nothing else will do. As a load descends on a foot, so the foot swells to take the strain. In working hard in this way with all the complex actions of flexing, rolling and springing, so it sweats.

Wool will take up sweat without complaint. Man made fibres will not. The result of this impossible absorption is a hot spot — the prelude to a blister. Even foot powders are conducive to blisters since they induce more friction between boots and foot than is necessary. The best relief for feet that have been worked hard is a stop, a rest and exposure to the open air. A dry pair of woollen socks restores new life into otherwise tired feet.

There are two distinct schools of thought about socks. One goes for one pair of thick, loop-stitched, nylon-reinforced socks of ankle length. The other inclines towards two pairs; one inner thinnish pair of fine wool with a thick pair of coarser knit over. These can be ankle length or knee length with the outer pair rolled down to form an anti-stone cuff over the boot as is the way with climbers.

Whichever method is adopted, the aim is to get a reasonably thick layer of wool over the foot, a layer without darns, loose ends, ruckles or tightness. A snug fit always.

With the boot undone, and the toes touching the toecap, there should be room in a well fitting boot to put a finger down behind the heel.

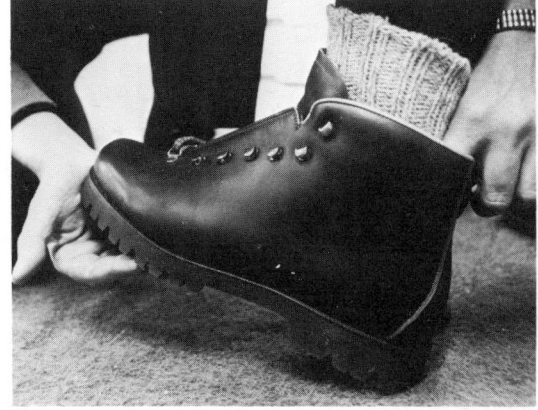

Once the socks have been bought, there comes the most important first step in backpacking — the hike to the boot shop. For those who live in big cities there is no hardship in this first important journey. Country dwellers, and those who live in smaller towns, have a bigger problem. There is no substitute however for going to an expert boot seller with a wide range of quality footwear specially designed for the walker.

In an expert bootfitter's hands the tyro backpacker's feet will be matched to the best combination of leather and bootmaker's skill. Price is the last consideration for the person with backpacking seriously in mind. Cheap boots spell trouble, although there are exceptional people who hike in plimsols and put up with the agony.

A good and properly fitted boot is a joy to wear once it is broken in. It offers a tough protection against the rough going and the projections which would penetrate ordinary shoes. The sole pattern gives a sound footing in slippery conditions. The cuff checks tiny stones from entering. The one piece upper gives protection from water and a lining provides some insulation against extremes of heat and cold. The lacing system snugs the boot down perfectly so the boot becomes an integral part of the leg — no sloppiness, no blood-stopping restriction; ventilation without voids.

An expert boot-fitter will ensure that the boots fit as well as possible before they are broken in.

These Scarpa Bronzo boots weigh just over 4lbs a pair. One piece construction and Vibram Montagna soles make them a good choice for the year-round backpacker.

There is much mystique about breaking in boots once they have been bought. Some can walk right out of the shop and keep walking. Others need weeks of preparation before that first hike can be attempted. Most people should reckon on being in the latter category.

Breaking in is merely a way of easing the leather to conform exactly to the shape of the foot. The stiffer the upper, the tougher the boot and the longer the process. Cheaper Italian soft leather boots are easy to break in but lack both comfort as they get older and sole thickness to prevent sharp stones from putting point loads on the soles of the feet.

There is no point in buying climbers' boots with stiffened insteps and which weigh four pounds or more. The greater the weight the greater the fatigue at the end of the day.

Boots need careful maintenance. They must be washed off after each trip, wiped out and left open to dry, and finally must be given a light coating of mineral dubbin to keep them supple and reasonably waterproof. Wet boots must never be dried close to a strong heat otherwise they crack and disintegrate. A little and often is the motto when using dubbin or proprietary oils.

Use of a double leather mid-sole in a good backpacking boot ensures that a worn out sole can be replaced. This resoled boot is a Robert Lawrie Mark XXXI R.

Our novice has now been fitted with better boots than his army surplus ones.

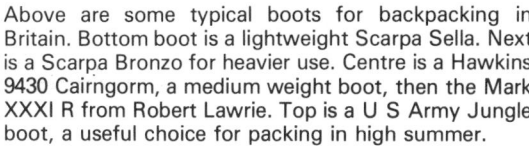

Above are some typical boots for backpacking in Britain. Bottom boot is a lightweight Scarpa Sella. Next is a Scarpa Bronzo for heavier use. Centre is a Hawkins 9430 Cairngorm, a medium weight boot, then the Mark XXXI R from Robert Lawrie. Top is a U S Army Jungle boot, a useful choice for packing in high summer.

Begin by walking around the house for an evening or so, then work up to several miles out of doors each weekend before leaving for that trip of a lifetime. Go armed with a packet of Dr Scholl's moleskin and a small pair of scissors at all times. At the first sign of local warmth on the foot, stop, make a patch of moleskin for the area and don't let a blister form if it can be prevented.

If a blister does form, nurse it immediately. A watery blister must be burst close to the rim and the water squeezed out before covering with moleskin and donning boots again. First though, examine the boot near the area of the blister — a loose thread, a spot of glue, a nail or a rucked sock is enough to bring enormous misery.

Forget about old soldiers' stories of soaking boots in warm water, donning them and walking them dry to break them in. This is savage treatment not only for feet but for good boots. Backpacking is for pleasure, not enforced route marching. Be sensible and walk yourself easily into this early phase of backpacking.

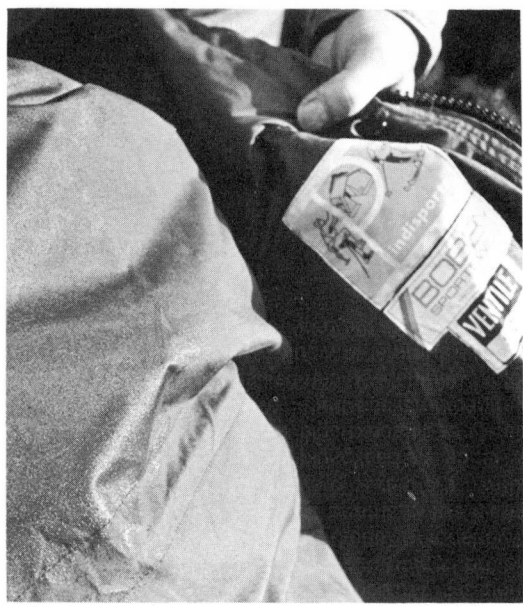

Condensation will form on the inside of any totally water proof clothing.

Fishnet vest, lambswool sweater and thick wool shirt form the backpacker's base clothing.

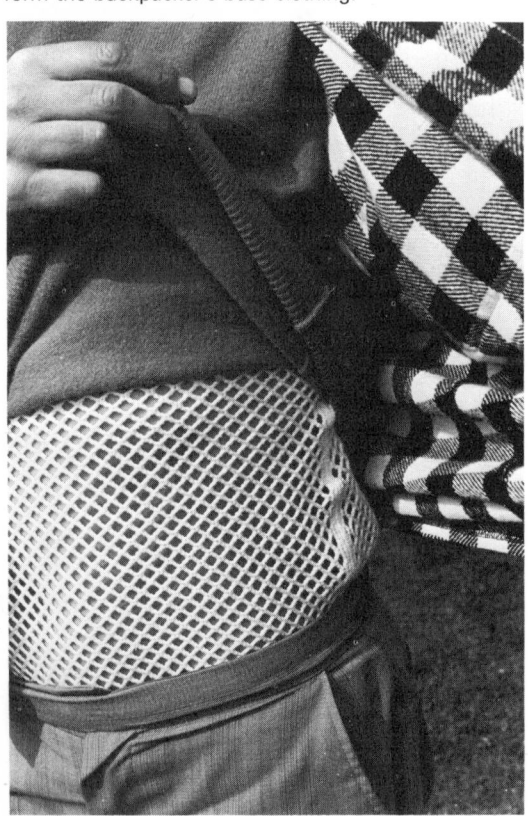

Working upwards from boots and socks, the backpacker has a rather special wardrobe to meet his requirements. As he walks along or lies snugly in his sleeping bag he must create a microclimate for himself to balance the weather outside. It is necessary however to understand the physiology of a microclimate before creating one.

A human body at work consumes food and turns it into nutrient. The nutrient is turned into heat, energy and water. The nutrient breaks down into carbonic acid and other substances which are washed away in the bloodstream through the kidneys into the bladder. The water must pass through the pores and find a way out to the atmosphere.

The water vapour is trapped by clothing which if it is not cellular will soon be soaking. A backpacker with wet clothing is at risk from exposure, so he must dress with this critical situation in mind.

The head, genital area and underarms are heat zones, and about half the body's heat loss goes by way of the head. If you want to keep warm, cover the head. If you want to keep cool, get air to all three zones.

Fishnet underwear is long proven for wear in both hot and cold climates and should be adopted by the backpacker. The trunk and lower body can be dressed this way by using *thick* cotton-mesh clothing; T-shirt and trunks. The netting makes tiny air cells through which the moisture can evaporate, and stands off the next layer of clothing to prevent it being soaked.

This is the only function of fishnet underwear. It is useless unless closely clad with a layer of wool through which the moisture can find its way to the air. Trousers should be woollen and close weave to prevent wind penetrating. There are specially made backpackers' trousers to varying designs which give roominess for the movement of legs and no gripping when climbing hard on a steep trail. The seat is sometimes made double with a layer of oiled silk between to keep the damp ground where it belongs. Because, as will be explained later, the better packframes have wide waist belts to take the load, backpackers' trousers are self-supporting so that no projections can cause painful areas. Front pockets are cut lower to allow hands to enter under a packframe waist belt and back pockets are flapped over to keep vital things from blowing away. Some trousers have a thigh pocket big enough to carry a one inch Ordnance Survey map.

Any good woollen trousers will do really, providing they are fairly thick, cut full and a bit baggy rather than being trendy. The addition of cuff tags fitted with Velcro so that they may be pulled up close around the ankle when the going is muddy is a useful modification.

Now the body is properly clothed with base clothing. Good boots over properly fitting woollen socks, trunk covered in fishnet underwear and

Our beginner has now put on a pair of Derby Tweed trousers from 'The Practical Camper', a Mountain Equipment down sweater and a Balaclava hat.

covered over with loosely fitting woollen trousers and closely fitting lambswool long-sleeved sweater.

To increase warmth add a wool shirt of coat length style with breast pockets, worn outside the trouser band. But never heavy sweaters which cannot be opened all the way down the front for ventilation when the going gets harder. For winter or out of season packing, most people invest in a down-filled waistcoat or light weight duvet with hood. This garment still allows body moisture to get out to the air yet keeps away the effects of strong wind. Duvet clothing has the advantage of being extremely light and compressible so that it is not a nuisance when it has to be carried in the pack. Knitwear is less good, being heavier for the same bulk and less compact to carry.

The 'Dalesman' jacket, from Mountain Equipment, is available with a filling of either down or dacron. The tough nylon outer shell will resist heavy showers, but dacron will retain body heat even if soaking wet, an advantage over down in British conditions.

Shell clothing has only one function. To protect the underclothing from being soaked by rain or penetrated by cold gale-force winds. Shell clothing should only be worn under such conditions for reasons which will become obvious in a moment. Modern shell clothing is made from nylon taffeta which has been made impervious to water by coating with a flexible plastic such as polyurethane. Because it keeps out rain it also keeps in body moisture vainly trying to get away from the pores, through the various cellular layers of woollen clothing, to evaporate on the surface. Fully waterproofed shell clothing prevents this happening. As long as the moist body air is warm it will not condense. However, once it strikes the inner surface of the shell clothing just a few thousandths of an inch from the colder atmosphere — an atmosphere which is high in humidity anyway — the body vapour turns to water. After an hour or so of hard going it is difficult to decide whether the shell clothing is leaking or not. The immediate reaction is to reject coated nylon shell clothing as useless, but this is short sighted. One gets wetter, quicker, by not wearing raingear, than by the effect of condensation inside the shell.

MOAC oiled cotton rainwear is as waterproof as nylon and can be used as a general purpose jacket.

The Henri Lloyd two-piece nylon rainproof suit weighs 1 lb.

The cagoule is the most basic form of backpackers' weather proof clothing.

Most backpackers have taken up the climber's cagoule — a smock-length coated nylon one-piece garment with an integral hood fitted with a draw string both around the hood face piece and around the skirt.

A better garment is the two-piece jacket and trousers of the same material. By unzipping the jacket some venting of the underneath can be made without too much water penetration from rain. Leggings or trousers have to be worn with both garments, so it is six of one and half a dozen of the other. The beginner can use a plastic mac and leggings until he gets the hang of things because specialist clothing is not cheap.

Gloves or mitts, and a balaclava complete the backpacker's wardrobe. If they are both wool, so much the better. A climber's balaclava with peak is best, and woollen mitts that are resistant to wind penetration beat gloves anyday.

The Robert Saunders Pakjak is a poncho that protects the hiker and his pack. Suitable for less windy areas, this garment resists condensation by providing greater air space. Between showers, it can be thrown open and tied up round the waist.

Good base clothing and raingear ensure protection in Britain's rapid changes of weather.

A down-filled sleeping bag weighing about 2 lbs is sufficient for backpacking in Britain between May and September. Here the size of a Mountain Equipment 'Lightline' (1 lb 15 oz) is compared to a roll of blankets.

The sleeping bag is really a piece of clothing which creates a microclimate. No one sleeping bag can suffice for all seasons and all latitudes. Thickness is warmth, no matter what creates that thickness. Providing it is cellular, and body moisture can find its way through to the open air, a sleeping bag could be filled with any material from wood chips, sawdust or steel wool to synthetic fibres or down.

Most sleeping bags the backpacker adopts are filled with down. The reason is simple. Only down can be compressed to a fraction of its original size and yet expand again to the full volume within minutes and go on doing this without collapse for years. Down is light in weight because it came from a bird which had to take to the wing and yet provide maximum insulation in all weathers.

Down can come as 'waterfowl down', and as a mixture of down and curled feather. These are the cheapest of the range. The finest is 'Northern goose down' which is very costly and in short supply. A bag filled with goose down will be very expensive and can only be justified for the serious backpacker going into winter weather or northern climates.

The bag shell is usually made from nylon or other synthetic fibres which have been glazed and have a high thread count to stop the down being lost through the fabric. They are cunningly cut in mummy shape with panels which are divided from one another by open weave fabric to prevent the down clumping together in one spot and leaving a cold area in another. Good bags have form fitting hoods which can be drawn up by cord. This saves heat loss from the head. Cheaper bags can be used if a watch cap of wool is worn in bed — the same balaclava hat which can be used on the trail during the day.

Some better class bags have zippers down the length of one side, with a down-filled flap on the inside to prevent heat loss through the zipper. The zipper should be double ended to allow venting from the bottom when the bag is pulled up.

It is a matter of personal preference whether a full form-fitting mummy bag is purchased, or a fuller bag which allows independent movement of the knees.

The principal differences are cost and weight to be carried, but after a hard day's hiking there is much to be said for having space for the legs to move independently to find a relaxing position in sleep.

For summer use, a down filled bag weighing no more than three pounds should suffice, but there are no hard and fast rules about this. A cold sleeper — that is a body with lower metabolism — will need thicker insulation to conserve the meagre body heat given off. A hot sleeper will be able to work with a much lighter bag and still sleep comfortably.

Before leaving sleeping bags, it is well to remember that down does need some care. It cannot abide being soaked and loses all its insulation value, whereas a synthetic fibre filled bag, even when soaked through, will retain a great deal of the original insulative properties. It can be wrung out and whirled around the head to drive some of the water out and then be entered for a reasonably comfortable night — the body's own heat will dry out the remaining dampness.

Synthetic fibres will not compress so densely as down, and the resulting bag weighs 10 or 15 per cent more than an equivalent down filled bag. No one yet knows the upper age limit of synthetic fibre filled bags so no comparison can be made on this score, but a good down bag given proper care will last a dozen years or more and still give good service.

For the initiate, it is best to look to a medium priced duck down and feather mixture filling for a bag weighing about three pounds. A hood is not necessary to begin with and the only essential quality is the construction which should be wall quilted or overlapping tube — never sewn through seams. A draw string around the mouth is necessary to close down the gap to prevent warm air loss.

Once the backpacking bug bites deeper the really finely engineered cold temperature bag with all the refinements can become an investment, while the older original bag can be used for overnight packing in high summer. It would be wasteful to buy this kind of bag before the requirement is established.

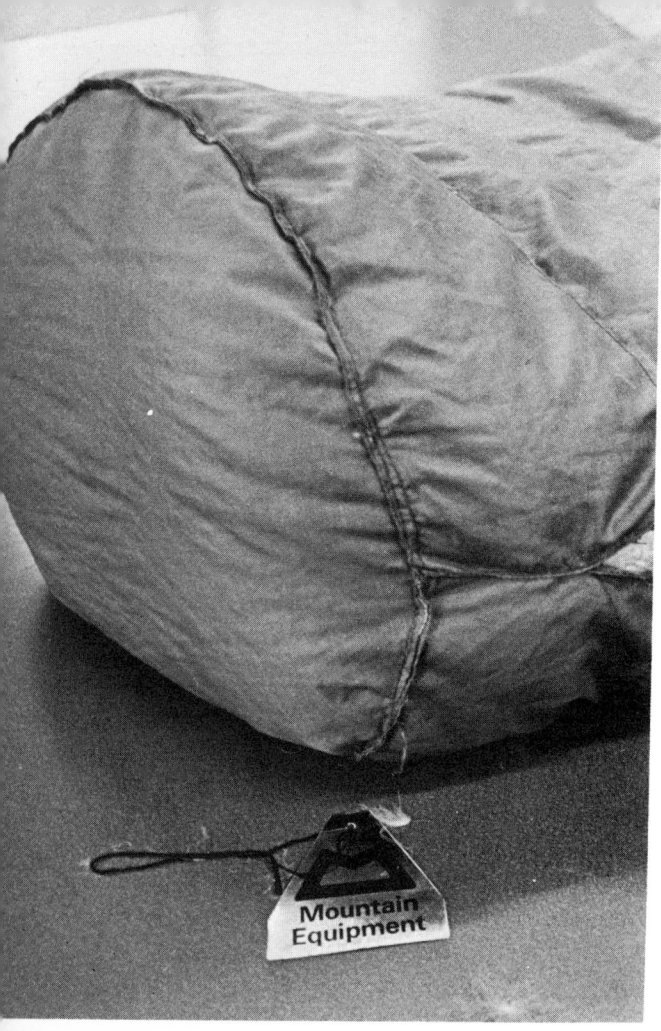
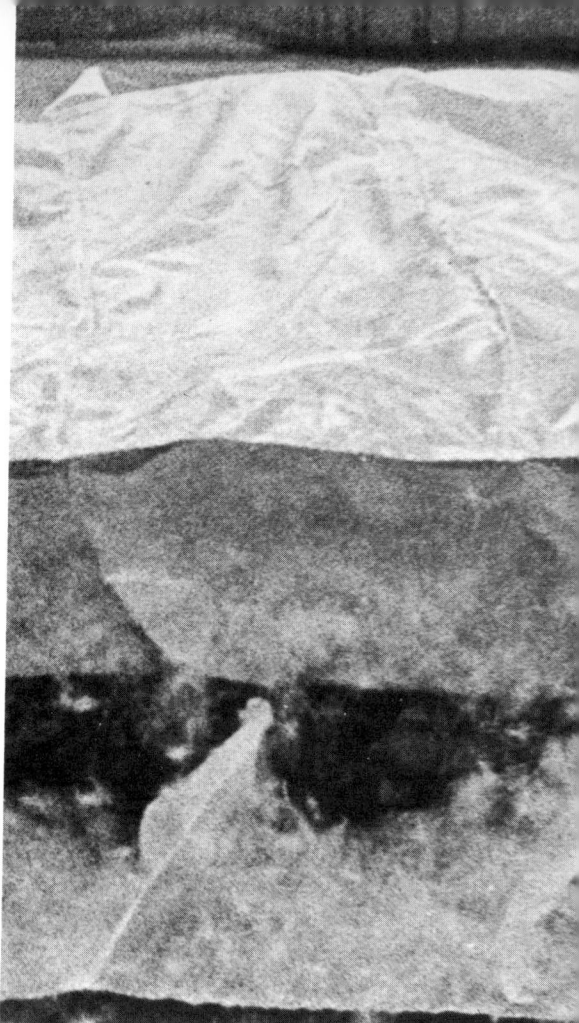

The down is kept in place by fabric baffles, either straightwall (below) or slant wall (above right). Both types allow the down to 'loft' fully, but slantwall baffling prevents any heat loss between the stitching lines. A boxed foot (above left) gives well insulated space for the sleeper's feet.

A sleeping bag's efficiency is determined by measuring its "loft", a term referring to the thickness a fluffed-out bag will achieve under its own expansion. That thickness is warmth — the wall of insulation which retains body heat without trapping body vapour given off during sleep.

Once a body lies inside a sleeping bag it follows that directly under the body the filling will be compressed to very nearly nothing. This compression opens a pathway for vital body heat to drain away. No matter what quality sleeping bag is purchased, the effect of compression under a sleeping body is always the same — a very cold spot.

The body loses heat very rapidly by conduction to the cold ground and since the earth is a massive heat sink the sleeping body never has enough reserve to heat up the ground to a point where comfort can be attained. The answer to this problem is simple and cheap. Every backpacker carries a piece of closed cell plastic foam on which he lies. In summer this pad is a mere 10 millimetres thick and just wide and long enough to stretch from the shoulders to just below the buttocks and wide enough to stretch from shoulder to shoulder. In winter a slightly thicker grade is used and it stretches the full length of the body from head to heel, tapering rather like a coffin lid.

This foam is fantastic insulation and balances off the loss which would normally occur through compression of the sleeping bag. To prevent it migrating in the night, most backpackers pop the foam pad under the ground cloth of the tent. If the pad is kept handy during the day it can also be used for meal and rest stops so that a good stretch out can be had without discomfort. However, the foam must be closed cell otherwise it will soak up water.

Of course there is very little mattress effect in this thin layer of foam. One should still kick a hip depression and a shoulder dent in the ground in the right position if one intends to travel as light as

Pitching a tent on top of dead bracken heads provides comfort and insulation. Tent is a Saunders Backpacker II.

The comfort-lover will not mind carrying the extra 1 lb 11 oz of a Brown Best 'Pakkabed' air mattress.

possible and use no other bed. The backpacker travels through the countryside with pride that he leaves no mark of his passing, so he makes no bower beds and pioneer rubbish like that. He might use dead bracken heads heaped together and then scattered again next morning, but that is about all. If he is as light a sleeper as the princess who felt a pea through several mattresses, then your backpacker takes along an air mattress.

This will give considerable comfort at the expense of more weight to be carried, and there is less insulation available in an air mattress to offset compression losses when compared with a foam pad. This said, there are some ingenious backpackers' air mattresses on the market. It is a matter of personal choice whether one is added to the inventory of equipment to be bought.

The mobile microclimate, achieved through proper clothing and sleeping bag with compression insulation, is completed with shelter. Although tents are a vital part of the packer's equipment, they are by no means essential. A large plastic bag having a wall thickness of 350 mil or more and big enough for a full grown man to be covered, is valid shelter. Indeed, there are many summer backpackers who travel extremely light who use no other shelter.

The routine in Britain is to lay out a sleeping pad, drape a plastic bag over and then spread out a sleeping bag over that. On fine nights the sleeping hours can be passed without further ado than counting a few stars and making out the

To pack a sleeping bag, take it by the foot and stuff it in handfuls into its carrying sack. The bag should never be rolled up.

The prevailing wind has shaped this tree. Wind is an exposure hazard to hikers.

In the morning, a sleeping bag should be laid out to air before being packed.

constellations before oblivion comes. The first spit of rain will fall on the face and awaken the sleeper.

Still in the sleeping bag, the feet are drawn up, the mouth of the plastic bag opened, the feet thrust down inside and when everything is covered over the plastic bag is drawn together loosely leaving as wide an opening as possible.

This vents some of the body vapour and prevents too much condensation and allows vital breathing air to reach the sleeper. This is the reason the plastic must have a wall thickness of 350 mil or more because its inherent stiffness prevents static electricity from cocooning and suffocating!

There is much to be said for sleeping under the stars without a tent roof. But in Britain we have to be realistic and remember we don't have a climate — only weather. Therefore, portable shelter in the form of a tent must be carried for more than the odd night away.

A group of backpackers pitch their tents in Wharfedale. From left, a Karrimor Marathon, a Saunders Lite Hike and a Saunders Backpacker II with Extreme fly sheet.

British lightweight tentmakers are probably the best in the world. They have embraced the problems faced by backpackers and offered ingenious solutions — some makers offering a whole range of solutions.

No one tent is ever ideal. How can it be? For the lone packer the solution might be the minimum volume of enclosed space. But after a few days this tiny envelope gets claustrophobic. A bigger tent weighs more and an even bigger tent to house two people can be advantageous in that the total weight of the tent can be shared in two smaller bundles.

Simple tents — bivouacs really — have only one thin skin of incredibly strong nylon fabric which has been coated with a waterproofing flexible plastic, just as with shell clothing. Cotton tents with only one skin used to allow internal water vapour, generated by the body and cooking, to find its way outside through the minute gaps between the threads. But cotton is heavy when compared with synthetics, and weaker too. It also rots more quickly, and lets in water if the walls are touched during rain.

In a tiny tent — a minimum weight tent — such restrictions cannot be accepted so synthetic fibres have ruled the day. But they have brought their problems — the biggest of which is the condensation dilemma.

Just as waterproof clothing "sweats" after a fairly short period of use, so does a man-made fibre tent. One either accepts this problem and adjusts the life-style to ignore it, or one adds yet more weight to find a way of eliminating it. The most successful way of eliminating condensation in a small tent is to make it with two skins — the inner being un-coated and the outer fully coated.

Vapour released inside the inner tent finds its way through the tiny untreated gaps of the inner tent fabric and then condenses as usual on the inside of the outer tent or flysheet. When enough moisture has been generated it runs down the inside of the fly and drops harmlessly onto the ground. At least that is the theory.

But experience has shown that while most of the better tents will do this for perhaps 80% of the time,

The Ultimate Bivouac tent. Weight 3 lbs.

A Saunders Lite Hike with Extreme fly sheet. Weight 4 lbs.

A Se-ab Expedition tent to sleep four. Weight 5½ lbs.

A Se-ab 'Original' two-man tent with extended fly sheet. Weight 5 lbs. (The sleeping bag is a 'Northern Lights' from Point Five.)

Some tents, such as the Karrimor Marathon, are designed to link to one another. This arrangement gives a covered area which can be well ventilated during cooking.

there comes a day of high humidity and the moisture forms on the inner tent also. Pushing the inner tent out of shape while asleep can cause moisture to be wicked back into the sleeping bag once it touches the streaming fly sheet. The result is a loss of insulation and a cold night.

Single skin tent makers try to overcome their problems with admitting as much venting air as possible. This works to a degree but some people object to the flow of air about them. Such extreme measures increase the need for a sleeping bag with higher loft than is necessary with a double-skin tent.

Tents for backpackers come in a wide variety of shapes too. The most common is a wedge with a head end higher than at the foot. Less common is the tube tent made with spring aluminium or glass fibre demountable hoops. This gives an impression of great space but suffers from an increased weight in hardware and single skin construction. The box tent has become fashionable recently and is by no means at the end of its development. Aerodynamically it is almost as stable as the wedge, can be coupled with others of the same size and make, and uses cloth more economically than the wedge with its complicated geometry. The pyramid tent, based on the old prospector's Baker tent, gives a two-skin construction to cover a ground area capable of housing four or more people. There is full standing headroom at the peak of the single centre pole. But weight is out of proportion to the comfort of such a layout.

Whatever tent is purchased, the tyro backpacker should see them all set up on grass at an outdoor showroom or better still, ask advice from others who have made purchases. The answers should be taken with a pinch of salt because no one admits to having bought a lemon.

Points to look for are legion. The floor tray should have either no seams at all, or at least seams that have been heavily doped to prevent water rising inside. The connection points at the corners should be examined carefully for water paths and security of corner pegs. The seams should be straight and parallel with stitches of fairly long length using polyester thread cased in linen which swells to fill the needle holes when wet. The guy lines should be attached in a way which allows renewal without major repairs. The sliders should grip smooth nylon cord without sliding involuntarily. The pole points should be reinforced and grommetted with brass rings. There should be a flyscreen inner door for closing off on hot nights when the insects are flying but still allowing cooling air to flow inside. Flyscreening should cover all other vents. A vestibule end is desirable to give covered storage space and an openable area for cooking in the dry. Reinforcing tapes should be sewn onto the stress points where guys will exert maximum pull to get a good set. Pegs should be aluminium and angular for maximum resistance to pull out in soft soil. The duffle bag should be the right shape to stow in a pack — long narrow parcels might be a neat way to wrap up a tent but are useless if stowed across the top of a pack when passing through undergrowth. A-poles give more freedom of movement at the entrance and are much more stable when the wind blows hard, but they weigh twice as much as two vertical poles for the same peak height. Colours vary widely from smart check designs to sombre olive drab or even camouflage. The latter are fine for solo hiking

The Hawley 'Barn' tent is roomy enough to sleep three, and has mosquito netting built in. Weight 7½ lbs.

Our backpacker begins to understand what lightweight means, as he replaces his 15 lb tent for one weighing 3 lbs.

through country where trails are not defined, and attract the least amount of attention from afar, but they are grim places to hole up in for a couple of days if the weather turns really nasty. Orange tents are used in the mountains and certainly shout the presence of a backpacker, but they give a splendid warm light even in the most torrential downpour. Blue tents also attract attention and they give some respite from hot sunshine on July days, but are dark places to live in when the sun isn't shining.

These are some pointers to look for. There are others such as the quality of a maker's zip fasteners, the way he cuts his cloth to waste or uses up scraps in the corners of wedge-shaped panels. These finer points come with experience. The main ingredient is, as with so many other things, a lot of commonsense. It is the packer who must carry what he purchases, and the true weight is not always what the manufacturer says it might be. And since ounces count, this weight factor is very real.

Ounces count and all add up to the total weight to be carried. There was a time when a lightweight tent was one that weighed six or seven pounds to house two with a squeeze. Then the first true backpacker's tents weighed in at under four pounds. The three pound tent was not long in coming and recently there have been some creations hovering around the two pound mark. But the average has settled at about 3 pounds 6 ounces for a two-man wedge and this is a good guide.

The enthusiastic backpacker collects a wardrobe of tents as the years go by. He has a hip pocket bivouac model weighing just ounces for his summer overnight trips, and his longer trip tent uses one inner tent with a light fly for summer and a full down-to-earth fly for winter camping. If he takes his family he uses another wedge for the children if they are around the age of 12, and perhaps a pyramid if they are younger, accepting the fact that young legs will limit the hike and so he can take more load over shorter distances to give greater comfort at night when supper is to be prepared and the children put to bed.

With reasonable care, a good tent will last many years and give much pleasure. Viewed in this way an investment of some £30 or £40 is not extravagant. While the best tents have fibres which are resistant to the deteriorating effect of ultra-violet exposure from the sun, some manufacturers take the view that a cheaper model of the same shape with no upper guarantee of ageing under the sunshine is preferable to some families of backpackers. It is a point worth bearing in mind when purchasing that first tent.

The maker's label is a good guide to the performance one can expect from a tent. A British maker's name usually guarantees satisfaction and aftersales service. A foreign label is asking for trouble. There are exceptions such as the excellent Swedish products which are marketed in Britain by a British company, but tents found in cut-price stores are not always happy purchases. Their origins are usually merchandising companies in the Far East cashing in on the boom in outdoor living, and usually there are no repair facilities in this country.

Now the backpacker has his portable home and his clothing, but it remains only disjointed equipment until it is all brought together and put into a pack which can be worn comfortably for mile after mile.

An all-night Force 9 gale in Yorkshire leaves a Karrimor Marathon and a Camp Trails Chaparral unharmed, although a peg has pulled out of the Chaparral.

Robert Saunders has recently enlarged his 'Base Camp' tent to give a greater sheltered area for cooking and storage.

In windy areas such as high moorland, the single skin straight-walled tents, pitched tail into the wind, come into their own.

Camping in a low-lying damp area calls for a double-skin tent with an Extreme flysheet to give adequate shelter and storage for all this party including the dog.

How to erect a single-skin tent

1. The Karrimor Marathon tent and poles in their carrying bags.

2. Fit the three section poles together.

3. Pull out the tent's tail into wind, and fasten down with two pegs.

4. Peg down the front of the tent door. Now the tent cannot blow away in the wind.

5. Carefully holding the top of each pole against the grommet in the tent fabric, insert the guyed pike through the grommet and into the pole.

6. Temporarily peg out the main guylines at 45 degrees to the door. Then raise the front of the tent with both poles simultaneously.

7. Remove the pegs pinning down the front of the tent and insert the bottom of the pole on each side.

8. Grasping each pole at the base, pull the tent floor straight until there are no wrinkles in it. Tighten the main guys.

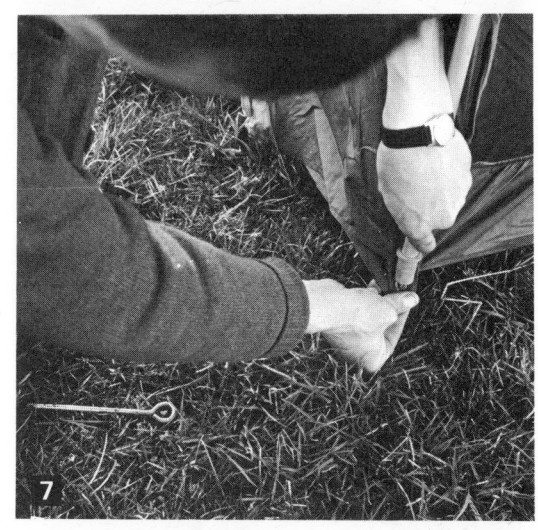

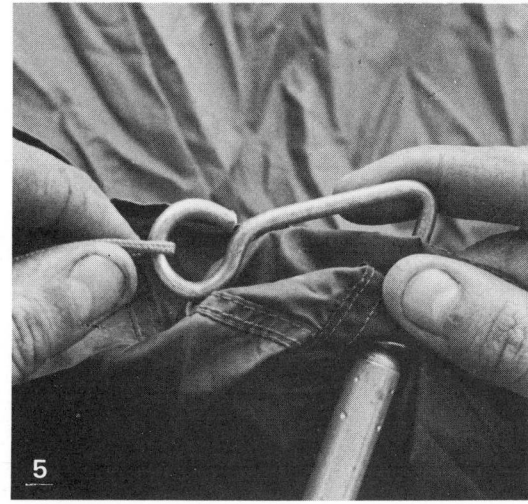

9. Pull out the tail of the tent and peg down, ensuring that there are no wrinkles in the roof. (The wrinkle in the photo will be cured by tightening the guy at bottom right).

10. Pull out and guy the roof panel. Peg out and clip the tent doors to the front roof panel. To save wear and tear on the ground sheet, slide a piece of 3 mm Karimat insulating foam under the tent before pulling out and pegging down the side guys.

11. The Marathon tent is now pitched, tail into wind, to provide sheltered cooking and sleeping space for two people.

12, 13. With a double-skin tent, the same procedure is followed, setting up the inner tent first. Fitting the flysheet in a high wind calls for control of the sharp pile on each pole. Carefully place the material over the pike and guy down the flysheet at the rear of tent before tackling the front end.

14. Peg down the front to hold the flysheet in place on the poles before setting out the sides on their rubber guy lines. The bottom picture on page 18 shows the erected tent.

Carrying loads of various weights has exercised human ingenuity since before time was recorded. There are examples of obscure methods still used in more primitive places. The tumpline — a rope attached to a head band worn around the brow — still exists in many parts of the world as a means of easing the burden of heavy loads. Early backpackers at the turn of the century explored the United States and Canada with devices which employed tumplines, but for the average packer they are obsolete.

So is the big steel-framed rucksack which was so popular in the 1930s. This monster often weighed six or seven pounds before anything was put into it, and like the dinosaur, it died because it could not compete with the more nimble and light weight sacks of today.

The famous Duluth sack of 70 years ago, with its framing of cane and simple webbing, still survives in some modern form. These sacks are the very least the modern backpacker can use for short trips demanding minimum weight and bulk to be carried. They now come in man-made fibres and are unsophisticated. There is one main pocket to the sack with perhaps two smaller side pockets — all three flapped over with a fly and secured with webbing tabs. The back where it is in contact with the body is sometimes padded with foam and given a covering with cloth which can allow body vapour to pass through and not form moisture over the spine. The shoulder straps are padded where they pass over the shoulders to ease the load over as wide an area as possible.

For the beginner, a sack chosen from the many in this range is the best way of getting started. Once the bug of backpacking bites deeper, nothing is lost for the sack makes a very good overnight carrier to run in company with the more sophisticated load carriers to be discussed in a moment.

The frameless pack, even at its highest development, is not for carrying loads much above 18 pounds. Anatomically, the body doesn't care for dead loads just sitting on the shoulders and since the load cannot be worn very high up with these frameless sacks the body develops a forward lean to counteract the ungainly weight placed upon it. This lean induces a lot more aches than are necessary.

To offset this in a small way, there is one dodge which can be tried. As well as wearing a pack on the shoulders, some of the articles can be put into a small waistpack which fastens around the top of the hips with broad webbing buckling at the front. When properly packed, this waist pack forms a shelf for the bigger shoulder pack to ride on. By slackening off the shoulder straps slightly the top of the bigger pack falls away from the body slightly and gives a bigger air space, while the main load is transmitted to the strong point of the body, the hips. Again though, the upper limit to this loading method is about 20 pounds. Such a method is ideal for those who want to combine walking with hitch-hiking to the trail. The

The Brown Best "Super Ariel" pack with pneumatic frame (1lb 2oz) is even more comfortable to carry when supported by a belt pack such as the Camp Trails "Vagabond" shown here. This combination allows transference of weight to the hips while doing away with the large frame.

two smaller sacks stuff more readily into a friendly passing car than the big frame sack which has become the true backpacker's main load carrier.

This framed piece of engineering was originated in the United States about 27 years ago. Using aluminium alloy tubing bent into a shallow S-curve with curved spacer tubes welded where the side tubes meet, the modern packframe transmits all the load onto three areas of the body — each shoulder and the hips. The shoulders merely offer a strong point to prevent the pack falling away backwards, and the hips carry the main part of the load.

Once an alloy packframe is correctly fitted to match size with the height of the wearer, packs can be fastened to the frame for carrying really enormous loads with some comfort. The average backpacker in summer carries about 25 pounds of irreducible load and about 1½ pounds of food for each day to be hiked and perhaps 2½ pounds of drinking water. For a seven-day trip then, the upper weight is around 45 pounds — a load which the good packframe with wide waist belt and big padded shoulder straps is emminently suitable for. But there are men of not unusual physique who start off on trips carrying 67 pounds and cover perhaps 15 to 20 miles in the first few days, gradually increasing this distance as the load diminishes with the food being consumed.

The Berghaus 'Dorsal' pack combines the waist and main packs into one close fitting canvas backed unit, made in two sizes. The large size has an internal frame of light alloy. The smaller size (illustrated) has a stiffener of insulating foam and is quite big enough to carry a two day summer load in its two compartments. Small sundries such as matches and first aid kit will fit into the side pockets of the waist belt which, by transferring weight to the hips, makes the 'Dorsal' comfortable to wear and excellent for summer hiking.

There are packframes and packframes. Since the original invention there have been many pirated ideas around the world. Each is subtly different although they all look the same at first glance. For instance, cheap frames are made from aluminium, not alloy. Consequently they bend and distort. Some frames are made with plastic compression joints and carried — a sort of crock of gold lure waiting at the end of the rainbow arc of each hike.

A handy guide of 45 pounds as an upper limit is valid. After the first trip with weights of this order, there starts a never ending quest by the backpacker continually to effect reductions in the total load to be

are not welded. This method has its protagonists. A properly welded joint should not break — being stronger than the parent metal — but a welded joint that fails far from expert help (ordinary blacksmiths are not usually equipped to weld aluminium alloy) means a ruined trip. The plastic compression joint on the other hand can be tightened with a simple tool. Parts can be replaced easily without sending the whole lot back to the manufacturer. Compression joints are cheaper to produce than good welded joints too.

The stiffness of the frame is very important. Unless compression joints are kept tight, or a poorly

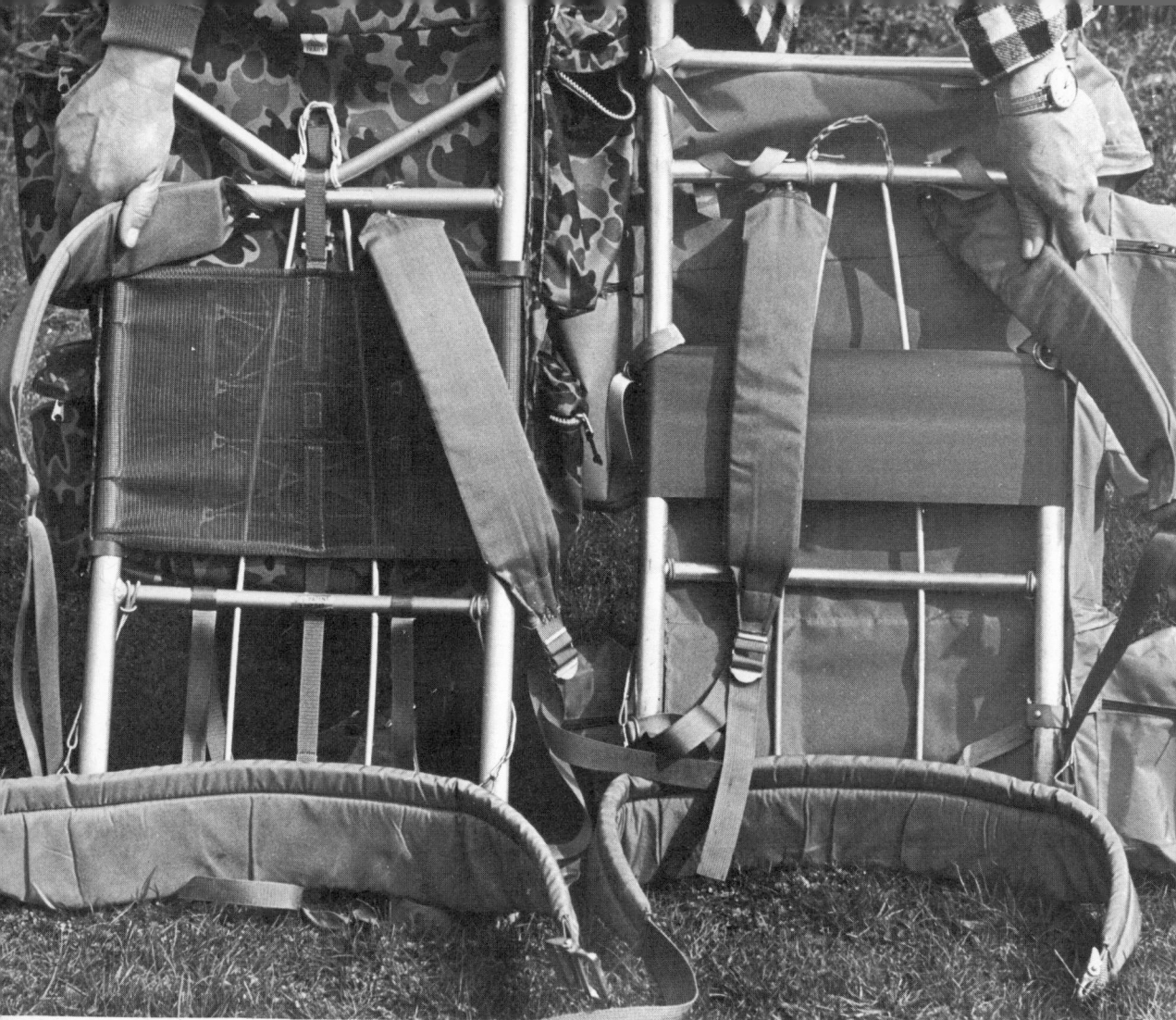

Two Camp Trails frames showing padded hip belts and shoulder straps. Left, a 515 Astral Cruiser frame, with a 575 Ponderosa bag fitted; the backband is nylon mesh, tensioned by a lace. Right a 501 Cruiser frame mounts a Brown Best 'Meridian' bag. The Backband is 5" nylon, tensioned by turnbuckle.

designed welded frame wrings under load, then energy is wasted to counteract the distortion. The best frames, therefore, have diagonal braces to stiffen them. These frames also have adjustments to the width of the yoke at the back where the shoulder straps fasten to the frame. This is most important, because unless a proper fit is achieved, misery follows.

The back must be protected from having the cross tubes digging into shoulder blades and in some frames the whole back is covered with nylon mesh which is tensioned with a running lace. This mesh allows the back to breathe away the moisture rising from hard worked muscles. Broad nylon webbing back bands are less satisfactory but if any of these wide bands cannot be tensioned right up — either with tiny turnbuckles or nylon laces — more misery is in store.

The big waist belt — it should never be less than 5 inches wide at the back and over the hips — is also a misery-maker unless properly fitted. When done up fairly tightly the belt should sit right over the hip bones and across the back of the pelvis — just over the point where the two natural dimples occur — with the buckle sitting low down the abdomen.

Failure to ensure this proper fit will probably restrict the blood supply to the legs and cause early fatigue. A properly fitted belt, on the other hand is a joy to wear. And if the shoulder straps merely lead downwards from the packframe and over the shoulders to anchor them in a wedging grip, the fit is perfect. Once the shoulder straps sag and hang right over the shoulders rolling will occur and this will induce early fatigue.

Final adjustment for fit can be made once the sack is fitted to frame, and load is applied.

Two bags by Karrimor fit the same Tote-em adjustable frame. On the left is the Randonneur pack for backpackers who like pockets. At right is an older model Tote-em Senior in cotton duck, without pockets. (Latest model Tote-em Senior packs have two pockets and can be obtained in nylon.)

Of course, since the good packframe is costly, there is no need to indulge in an equally expensive pack for the first season. Securing the load stowed in waterproof nylon stuff sacks to the frame with either a lashing or narrow webbing is perfectly acceptable backpacking practice. It may look unsightly and be less handy to reach everything once the load is packed but it does have the advantage of distributing all the bits and pieces into small units each in their own sack which can be taken inside a small tent. A big pack with all its pockets and gadgets does make packing much easier but it also takes up a lot of precious living space inside a small tent.

A good pack, properly wedded to a fitted frame, is very satisfying. The modern pack is made in tapering form — wider at the top — with enormous strength, plenty of properly dispersed pockets each with a plastic non-freeze zipper and variable closures to accommodate different loadings.

The materials of modern packs are tough man-made fibres which have been coated to make them water-tight. Unfortunately, every time the sewing machine needle passes through the cloth it makes a water path. So there is no such thing as a fully waterproof pack, no matter what the manufacturers might claim. Perishable and water

sensitive items are wrapped in polybags to prevent damage.

But more about packing in a moment. Styles in packs are very varied to suit the many different methods of loading. Everything in backpacking is a very personal matter and the manufacturers have sensed this vicissitude among the fraternity and traded on it. The result: deep packs, short packs, one bag packs, seven pocket packs, compressor packs that can be laced up smaller, two floor packs, freighter packs, and so on, ad infinitum.

What the newcomer must decide for himself before buying is how his own personal lifestyle will fit in with backpacking. If he is fastidious, then he will need lots of outside pockets. If he is a largely untidy person, then maybe the one bag sack with just one or two outside pockets will be just fine.

The main sack compartment on some sacks is made with a floor about half way down. The corners of this floor close to the back of the bag have triangular holes relieved in them. These holes accommodate tent poles in the vertical position close to the back. The lower main compartment is capacious, but the top much larger. The two main outer pockets are the higher sections and the smaller are below. Behind is a flat pocket covered by the fly.

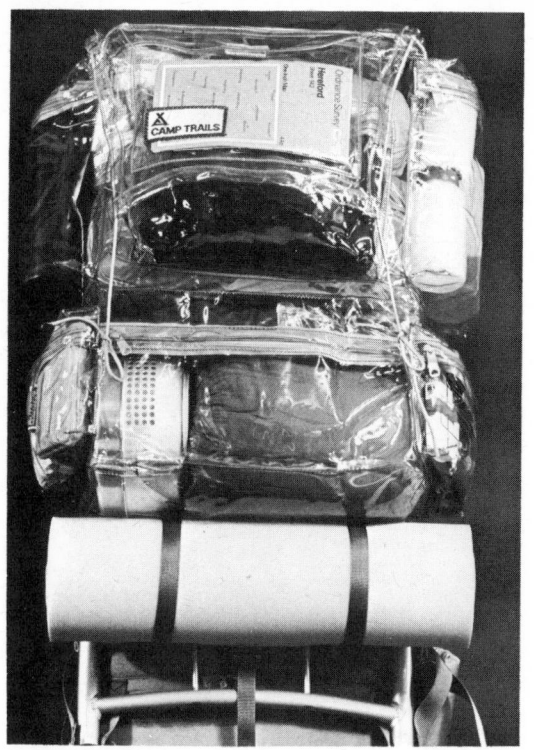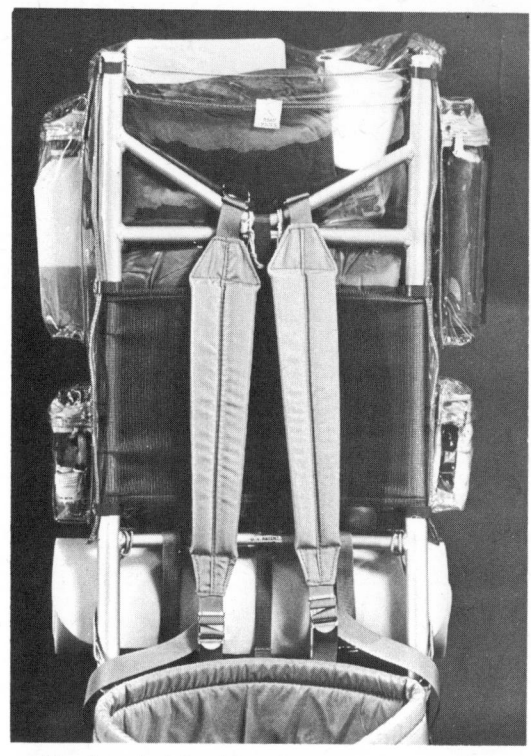

Packing, while remaining a matter of personal choice, is governed by the principle of 'heaviest objects as high up, and as near the spine, as possible'. Load shown here is for two days in summer, so a separate stuff sack is not needed for the sleeping bag which goes into the top compartment.

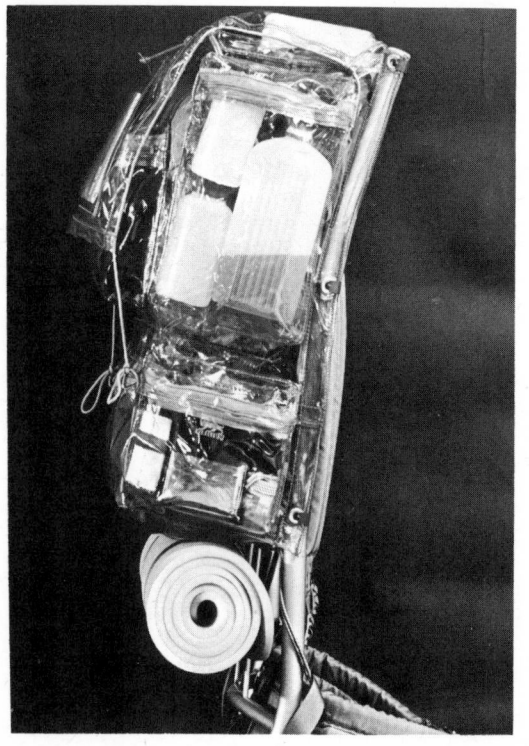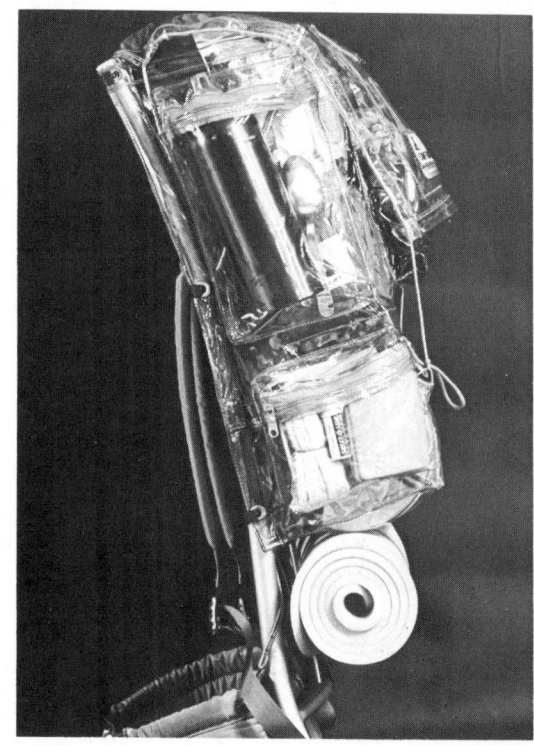

All these points are deliberate to facilitate loading which is a bit of an artform in its own right. The object is to get all heavy items as close to the spine as possible and as high up as possible. This distribution brings optimum comfort.

Into the lower main compartment goes cooking gear, spare clothes and other bulky but light items. Into the upper main compartment goes food, and shelter, while the upper outer pockets carry water and spare fuel for the cooking stove. The lower pockets carry trail snacks, flashlight, wash kit, first aid pack and stuff like that. The outer rear pocket takes up the wet weather shell clothing and spare socks.

Then, in a separate stuff sack which is lashed onto the lower part of the packframe, the foam sleeping pad is rolled up and slipped inside and made to uncurl to leave a void which is filled by the sleeping bag in its own stuff sack with the mouth at the opposite end.

The best way to get proper weight distribution is to lay the sack on a table with the side nearest to the shoulders on the table. The heaviest gear is laid inside first according to the loading plan outlined above, then on the next layer go the less weighty items and so on until the whole space is taken up and no voids are left which will allow gear to slop around.

The rest of the pockets can be filled without trouble, but it is a good idea to devise a loading plan and then stick to it because it becomes habit to reach for a certain pocket knowing that a párticular item will be found there.

Now a fully loaded pack sack is a cumbersome thing until hoisted on the shoulders. There is an art to this too, and it should be done in the sequence shown opposite with care not to bump the pack down on one corner of the frame once it is removed. For really heavy loads above 50 pounds, the accepted way of manning a pack is to stand it on a surface slightly higher than a crouch position and then back into it leaning forward as the load is taken before securing the waist belt.

The waist belt should be settled in exactly the right position and cinched down as tightly as possible with the shoulders slightly hunched up. This will take the direct load off the belt stays for a moment while the belt is tightened. Then standing upright, the buckle should be pulled right down the abdomen until all feels comfortable. The last act is to ease down on the shoulder strap tabs until the shoulders are wedged firmly but without constriction into the pads.

The care with which adjustment of the right sized pack frame is necessary now becomes apparent. If the load is wiggled from side to side and swayed at the same time, any looseness which could be troublesome later shows up immediately. Adjust accordingly until the shoulderstraps stop the rolling. Feel carefully for anything hard in the pack which might be poking into the back. Tighten up the

Here is one method of putting on a pack. Lift it from the ground and rest it on a knee (above). Then put one arm through the shoulder strap.

Sling the pack onto your back and put the other arm through (above left). Lean forward, to take the pack weight off your shoulders and fasten the hip belt (below left). Stand upright, allowing the hip belt to take the pack weight, and tighten down the shoulder straps.

backbands until the whole load is clear of the back.

Now walk around a little and see if there are any rattles — nothing is more annoying than a rattle that keeps sympathetic time with each stride. Identify the rattle, take the pack off and sort it out. On some packs — especially American packs — the pack is attached to the frame with clevis pins and circlips. These circlips can flap around and tap, tap on the frame. This is the source of another annoying noise that can get a backpacker down on a long boring section of a trail. Some packs squeak as they move on the wearer's back, but most people seem to think this is a friendly noise.

Always have a spare clevis and circlip — attaching one to a zipper pull is a good idea — especially the clevis used to join the bottom of frame to the bottom of the shoulder straps and the waist belt and the short pin to join shoulder straps at the top of the frame. These four pins are vital. A couple of paper clips in a pocket make first aid circlips if they become lost.

It will take some time to get used to pack and load. Some packers use "medicine packs" — sand bags of ten pound loads which can be put into a sack in increments for practice hikes near to home. This incremental practice loading teaches a lot about balance and stride with a load on the back. It also searches out weaknesses in boots which have yet to finish being broken in. It is better to find out such shortcomings on a short hike near home than on a much dreamed of holiday later on.

Lengths of chain which weigh known amounts can also be used as dummy loads and they lie inert in the pack once loaded.

There are some dos and don'ts about big packframes and sacks. They should be properly worn on flat or moderately steep tracks. On descending a steep track the shoulders need to lean back and the weight shifts its centre of gravity. It is then better to free off the waist belt until the flat is reached.

On crossing lodge pole bridges or rock piles over stream beds in spate, a pack should be freed off and either carried in one hand and balanced or carried in front by hugging the load. To lose balance and fall into water is a nasty and dangerous experience with a pack still attached to the body. Naturally one would sink like a stone in deep water or even get jammed under a tree trunk and drown if the straps are still fastened.

Never jump down even moderately small heights with a loaded pack on. It can cause sprained ankles and compression fractures of the spine. A better way is to lower the pack over a ledge and then scramble down to the pack afterwards. A short length of parachute cord is a useful packer's odd bit of gear. There are many other uses for a piece of cord of this weight having a length of say 30 feet.

The pack straps must be properly adjusted to avoid unbalancing the walker on steep slopes or rough surfaces.

When crossing an obstacle, it is best to take off the pack and put it down on the far side rather than try to cross while wearing the pack. This stone wall is in Wharfedale.

Only if you are completely sure of your footing should you attempt this sort of climb when carrying a pack. These steps are beside the Brecon Canal.

Taking the pack off at the end of a long day leaves one with a marvellous sense of freedom and lightness; rolling like a horse is optional.

When trying to get through stiles and other small gaps, take off the pack and feed that through first before attempting to get through. There are cases on record of packers who have become wedged and unable to move one way or the other.

And get a fully laden pack off the back for a few minutes each hour. It makes the world of difference to the length of hike that can be accomplished in any one day. A pack propped up against a wall or against a hiking staff makes a fine back rest for a "hoo harr" on hard trails.

Now the backpacker is complete except for food and water and some means of providing portable fire on which to cook. But before discussing pots and pans and stoves, it is better to consider food. After much consideration here in the kitchen department it will be possible to make an intelligent choice of stoves and pans. Blindly to buy a stove of one sort or another without considering diet is wasting money on a very costly item.

Having dressed the packer, given him shelter and a bed, we now have to feed the brute. This is more complicated than it sounds. The backpacker at work is a thermo-machine using fuel and giving in return a certain quantum of work energy. Calories are most important to ensure the bio-machine burns on long enough to accomplish the tasks he has set for himself, no matter what the weather. Weather has a lot to do with food for the colder it gets the more calories are needed to make up for heat losses.

There are some gourmets of the trail who can contrive cordon bleu cookery from a few dehydrated packets of food to a haphazard menu, but they are rare and not especially wise. Everything which has to be carried should only have a place in the pack if it forms an essential part of the whole trip. Food brought home is weight carried to no avail. It is true there should always be an emergency meal to hand, but no more than that. Therefore, a trip is planned in detail, not only on maps but in the kitchen long before the start of a trip. Each day's rations are stripped of all extraneous packaging and portioned out in meal-sized portions before repacking into the ration bag.

A selection of backpacking foods, both specialist and general use. Most of these can be bought in a supermarket.

It is possible to live consistently off a basic ration, but variety in the diet adds considerably to the enjoyment of a trip.

Generally speaking, the backpacker eats to live. His whole menu is aimed at the easiest possible preparation to provide the best possible food value. Waste has no place in the pack. Calories are needed to give work energy, but they soon burn off and leave a tired hiatus until the next meal break. So carbohydrates have to be heavily supplemented with fats. Protein is essential too, but not as much as many people imagine.

In summer, on medium trails below the treeline, a backpacker needs about 3,000 calories. Colder weather, higher altitude and exposure bump up this requirement to even as much as 5,000 calories a day, but for shortish trips a figure of about 3,500 calories is a good guide for the average person of medium build — the classic mesomorph. Thin people, tall people, will need more. Stouter people can do with less, for in every pound of human fat there is about 2,800 calories and this is used up if there is a slight deficiency in the diet. Too little food will bring early fatigue during the day, and restless sleeping at night.

Sugars, honey and candy are quick sources of calories. Their lift in energy is experienced immediately by a tired man, but these sources of calories soon burn away.

Grains and cereals are more sustaining sources of calories but these need digestion to release their full energy quota. Although fats burn a long steady flame in the muscles, too much fat revolts the stomach especially when the body is working hard.

There must therefore be a balanced all round diet which matches the body's needs. Since every one's tastes are different, the actual composition of a menu is entirely personal, but here are some pointers. Supper should begin just after breakfast and go on steadily all day. A single blow-out meal is useless to a backpacker. He has neither inclination to prepare and eat it nor does his stomach want to cope with such a vast amount of food at one go. During sleep the body turns down the throttle and asks for only a tickover trickle of food, so it is quite wrong to eat a big meal just before turning into a sleeping bag in a dog-tired state.

Nor does breakfast have to be a large meal, but it should be adequate to sustain that first breakaway in the morning after camp has been struck and the pack shouldered up. All the time the body is at work it is consuming much water to make up for the evaporation losses through the pores and the throat.

Many packers make up a ration of food based on Swiss breakfast cereal in its many proprietry forms. This base material is supplemented with wheat germ for vitamin E, extra sugar in the form of glucose powder, dried fruit and honey coated nut. Some add chocolate scrapings made with a potato peeler on

Bagging up at home gets rid of unnecessary packaging and allows you to premix the right quantities of food, with additions of your own. Here Muesli is being fortified with more raisins, sugar, chocolate and some dried milk.

plain chocolate. Three four-ounce portions of this concoction will give a base supply of about 1,500 calories a day. It can be eaten with fresh milk if available, condensed milk from a squeezy tube or even plain water — warm or cold. Plain muesli is a good additive to soup mixes as a bulker and since breads have no place in the packer's larder, muesli fills the bill admirably. Muesli also has just the right amount of "fullness" about it without producing a bloated feeling; it sticks to the ribs a long time after being consumed. Being almost inert in its dry state, it doesn't spoil with heat and can tolerate as much bumping around in a small polybag tied at the neck as you care to give it. Since muesli mixes in the various personal forms need no cooking, valuable fuel which has to be carried in the pack is saved — less weight need be carried.

Of course, a diet of muesli mixtures is boring, so it must be supplemented with other foods. Eggs form the best, quickly cooked and rapidly assimilated form of protein available. In ordinary weather, eggs will keep reasonably well for several days on the trail and can be found for sale even at remote farms and tiny country stores. The egg has one big disadvantage — it is easily broken. No matter. Break them at home, one at a time into a cup until half a dozen eggs, with their whites almost intact as a large transparent envelope, can be poured into a small wide-mouth poly bottle with screw cap. In this way they will not suffer from breakages and yet can be poured one at a time into a pan for poaching, frying, coddling, scrambling, omelette making and just about every other use but boiling. Boiling an egg is wasteful of precious water and heat and is therefore a luxury.

Fats come in many shapes and forms. Plain butter is too limited in scope for the backpacker. It is easily polluted with sand, dirt and other foods, it runs away in the slightest heat and is altogether unsatisfactory.

Eggs are easy to cook and easy to carry, shelled, in a polybottle. A non-stick frying pan weighing 7oz by Optimus is being used over a Trangia cooker.

Cheese is a much better form of fat, while cooking oil is easy to carry in a small poly bottle. Salami is fat-riddled and tasty; precooked streaky bacon wrapped in foil with all its fat is appetising even when eaten cold. Peanuts eaten as a trail snack provide a good source of second-class protein and much fat.

Breakfast should be taken leisurely in stages, starting in the sleeping bag with a large mug of hot sweet tea, followed by dried fruit which was simmered after soaking the previous evening and set to cool in the doorway of the tent. Then it is time to get up, and have a wash and tidy up. After the sleeping bag has been set to air, it is time for another cup of tea and maybe some scrambled egg and a helping of muesli. Or it might be a cheese omelette.

After packing up and striking camp, lunch starts with a handful of peanuts nibbled as the first hard strides of the day begin to wear into a rhythmic pattern. Candy bars cut into slices make good rest stop snacks and fruit juice crystals dissolved in a canteen of water slake mounting thirsts. At lunch break a bowl of soup is welcome, thickened with a little muesli to give it a satisfying body. So the day progresses until camp is made and another mug of tea brewed.

Supper is again leisurely, with perhaps a curry of some sort followed by a chunk of cheese and perhaps some sultanas eaten right from the hand. A bedtime drink of chocolate or cocoa laced with condensed milk is very pleasant. Don't forget to stew

Fresh sausages make a fine start to a walking weekend, and need only a little cooking oil.

It is best not to cook inside a tent unless it is adequately ventilated, because of fumes from the stove, and condensation from the steam. Here two Karrimor Marathon tents were linked, and a light breeze through the open doors carried the steam out. Stove is an Optimus 99 petrol stove with windshield and cover/pan.

Walking can be a thirsty job. Beer is a food, as well as a drink. Who needs an excuse, though?

off the fruit for morning on the same flame as heated the water for cocoa. Then a rinse of the mug, a pan of water set ready for the morning tea and it is bedtime. During the day the 3,000 calories have been consumed without being noticed.

You will notice there has been no mention of meat, potatoes, vegetables, bread, cake or any of the things we use at home. The reason is simple enough: none of these things are worth packing on the back for they either need much fuel for their cooking or they soon go stale and lose their appeal and food value. Dried meat, and meat substitute made of soya, are available in single and bulk packs, to be reconstituted when required. Plenty of dehydrated products are also on the market to provide instant mashed potato.

It will be noticed too, that all the packer's diet can be prepared quite quickly on a simple single burner stove. Mostly the cooking entails so little work that washing up is merely a wipe around the pan with a piece of kitchen paper and a swill of water after. This too is deliberate.

Nor has any can been mentioned. Canned goods weigh too much for the value of their contents, although there are some exceptions. Some fish is packed in aluminium cans and these are taken for curry making or simply eating out of the can on a rainy day when it is best to stop in the sleeping bag and rest up.

But such things as baked beans, canned tomatoes, canned fruit juices and the stuff we eat without thinking at home become drudges on the trail when everything needs to be carried — and, it must be emphasized that empty cans must be carried home again for proper disposal.

The exceptions are canned meats to make a meal early on in the trip, and perhaps a can of fruit in heavy sweet syrup which is a rainy day morale boosting luxury.

Fresh foods do have their place. Milk should be consumed wherever it can be found. Eggs have been mentioned and fruit in season — particularly apples and maybe the odd orange eaten along the way without even finding its way into the pack. Fresh meat is delicious cooked on a kebab stick over a small open fire if one is permitted. A piece of gammon or cooked ham bought in a country store and consumed that day adds zest to the diet. Generally though, everything is planned right on the kitchen table and bagged up before the start of a trip. This leaves nothing to chance and ensures a properly balanced diet which should have been completely eaten by the return to base.

Some country pubs also put on quite good bar food, and this is appropriate backpacking fodder. It takes no heat to prepare and might be the social opening to finding a good camp site for the evening. But beware of consuming more than a couple of drinks in cold weather — it reduces the body's ability to cope with the cold. More about this later.

Professor Yudkin the dietitian maintains that white sugar is useless stuff, and most experienced backpackers will agree with him, preferring honey and unrefined brown sugar in its place. Honey can come in squeezy tubes these days and this is a good way to carry the sticky stuff without spilling in the pack. Condensed milk has been available in tubes for a long time, and now there are chocolate sauces and jams in them too.

In the United States, the backpacker has a vast range of special foods prepared in packets to which he only has to add water, and in some cases cook for a minimum while. They are available to a lesser degree in Britain too, but are expensive. In most cases the backpacker in Britain can find everything he needs on the shelves of the nearest supermarket. Only accelerated freeze dried stews are hard to find and fortunately most special food makers supply one of these. Curries, pasta dishes and dried egg concoctions are best provided by mixing things up for oneself.

One indulgence the experienced backpacker carries in his larder is dried herbs. A tiny amount of marjoram or basil makes ordinary foods more exciting. Eggs turned into omelete fine herbe can be part of any backpacker's repetoire if a few herbs are carried in a tiny plastic sachet.

Some backpackers, mindful of weight and idle in their cooking, have been known to restrict much of their diet to invalid food in powder form which either needs only water added, or is used as an additive to other liquid foods. For those who can stomach this sort of thing, it can be an extremely convenient way of carrying concentrated food in an easily prepared form.

The experienced backpacker is for ever looking for new ways to keep his load to be carried down to the minimum weight and yet provide him with the maximum return in food value. Even so, the best of the backpacking fraternity cannot reduce their loads to much less than 1½ pounds of food a day and stay fit for more than a couple of days at a stretch. This basic loading is significant and should be remembered when it comes to packing for the big trip. Few can carry more than two weeks' food on the shoulders, nor is there need. Savings should always be made in the main kit and not on food. Good food is good news to a hungry man on the trail.

It can be seen, now that we have discussed food, that providing a heat source for backpacking cooking is entirely different from the urge to go out and buy a stove. Stoves are fascinating pieces of engineering and have an appeal in their own right. This appeal should not be indulged — rather the hard economics of the need to carry portable fire should be examined.

The simplest portable fire is a box of matches. With these fire starters a small open fire can be raised, if such a luxury is allowable. Unless permission to light an open fire has been granted by the landowner, most open fires are ruled out — other than perhaps on the beach where firewood abounds, and ownership is usually vested in the Crown. Here, unless there is some risk of setting fire to some farmer's land, an open cooking or warming fire can be enjoyed with very little problem, other than the usual drawbacks of any open fire.

Most people build fires far too big for cooking, and everyone suffers from streaming eyes as the smoke chases the cook from one position to another.

A stove, while expensive in terms of outlay and upkeep, is much more reliable and discreet. It has all the advantages of an open fire and only the dead weight of the stove and fuel as a disadvantage.

Stoves can be divided into four main groups, and one other group of novelties. These are petrol stoves, paraffin stoves, LPG stoves and methylated spirit stoves, with warmers burning solid fuel in stick or jelly form forming the other group. The latter are of no real use to the backpacker, so we must concentrate on the better forms of stove. For instance, methylated spirits is widely used as a fuel, and some stoves of this type are designed to include cooking pots and a windshield.

The modern Scandinavian spirit stove has much to recommend it. There is no need for pre-heating and the fuel is not explosive or volatile. The main drawbacks of the alcohol stove are the uncontrollable flame — a flame that gets hotter as the spirit vaporises — and the cost of the fuel. It works well at altitude and low air temperature, but it is thirsty. Supplies of fuel are not easy to come by in out of the way places.

The most popular of all portable fires is the ubiquitous LPG stove. Burning either butane or propane gas sealed up in a handy container the LPG (Liquid Petroleum Gas) stove is cheap to buy and can be lit merely with a spark for instantaneous ignition. Running costs are high, and for butane, the most common type, the efficiency drops off considerably with falling air temperature until at

A variety of stoves are available for the backpacker. Left to right, front row: the ½ pint paraffin burning Radius, and the new gas cartridge Vango S 7000 which since this picture was taken, has undergone design changes to avoid a patent infringement. Centre row: the SVEA 123 petrol stove, the Meta 71 cup, lid and stand, with fuel tablets in front, and the petrol-burning Optimus 99. At the back is the latest from Vango, a two-burner stove (S 7300) which works off any gas cartridge.

freezing it hardly works at all. The flame is 'lazy' and doesn't take kindly to drafts so an efficient windshield must be carried to complement the stove. It is essentially a summer tool for short term use, and its gas canisters must be carried around both full and empty if litter is not to be left behind. The design of most of the stoves tends to be unstable on uneven ground due to the problems of design which requires the burner to stand above the gas reservoir. There are exceptions and one unit has been designed to run on most gas canisters and it sits very close to the ground when ready for use.

The evergreen pressure stove can be divided into two main groups — petrol and paraffin burning. Paraffin stoves are very economical in their use of fuel and enjoy a big following among the older fraternity of backpackers. Paraffin taints everything

it touches however, and can easily leak out into the pack and spoil a whole kit. Small amounts of fuel are harder to come by than petrol, and being less volatile than petrol, paraffin has to be pre-heated to make it vaporise. This pre-heating means another item has to be carried around in the pack — spirit in liquid, jelly or tablet form.

The petrol fired stove comes closest to being the backpacker's ideal source of portable heat. The fuel is obtainable almost everywhere — even a passing motorist might be able to help — and it is quite economical.

Petrol fired stoves are robust and therefore heavier than most. They can be cranky and dangerous if not maintained in a fair order. They give off carbon monoxide fumes and should never be used in confined spaces without plenty of ventilation.

Above left
The Trangia cooker comes complete with pots and a frying pan lid, and uses methylated spirits.

Below left
First of the gas stoves, the Bleuet S 200 works off a Camping Gaz or similar cartridge. The tent in the background is an Ultimate U-2 Hoop tent.

Above right
The Turmsport burns meths, folds very flat, and has a controllable flame.

Below right
This is the smallest petrol-burning stove of all — the Borde 'Bombe', with a home-made windshield/pot-stand.

The lighting sequence for a petrol stove begins with opening the fuel filler cap to ensure there is sufficient fuel, and to release the air pressure from the last burn.

Fit the key over the regulator tap and turn it anti-clockwise to open the valve.

Warm the base of the stove by holding a lighter or piece of burning paper underneath, until petrol wells out of the nozzle (see picture) and down the stem into the cup. When the cup is full, turn the key clockwise to close the valve.

Now set the stove on a firm base with the pot supporting legs spread outwards or inwards to suit the size of the cooking pot. Leave the key on the tap for now.

Light the petrol in the cup, to heat the top burner plate and to pressurise the fuel tank.

As the yellow flame dies down, open the regulator valve with the key; the flame will turn blue, and the stove will start to roar. Adjust the flame as required, and remove the key from the regulator — it gets hot.

These disadvantages apart, the petrol stove delivers a wide range of heat from extremely hot to a mere glimmer. The best stoves have self pricking devices and now come with a complementary canteen of cook pots and windshield. Start-up is relatively simple once the hang of the routine is mastered. A little hand warming around the reservoir with the valve open will drive up a small quantity of fuel which dribbles over into a small pre-heating cup. The valve is shut and the fuel ignited with a little care. Very soon the valve can be opened and the burner roars into life. Spare fuel must never be carried in plastic bottles — special aluminium alloy bottles with screw caps and neoprene sealing rings are sold for the purpose.

An efficient windshield saves enormous quantities of fuel and one can be made very easily from four bicycle spokes and a small area of light cotton. The spokes are forced into the ground and a three sided shelter is formed behind which the stove can find shielding.

Before leaving portable fire, it might be a good idea to mention matches again. Every backpacker tends to take several packets disposed in places around his pack. Each box is waterproofed to the best of his ability against the dreaded possibility of having all his matches spoiled with water. A more efficient reserve fire-making idea is to stow a small plastic cigarette lighter in the pack. This will light even after falling into water and will provide some illumination in emergencies when a flashlight has failed.

More about emergencies later. The main things are now put together in the ring — the expensive chunks of foundation material with which to go backpacking. There remain such items as a knife, a dessert spoon, a drinking mug, a washkit, a compass, a whistle perhaps, sunglasses — a rabbit foot even — to be collected.

These oddments are very personal and are usually carried without regard either to original cost and real need or to weight. For instance, a knife will probably rank high on a backpacker's list of personal possessions. He may collect several until he finds a favourite. This final knife will be an expression of that backpacker's inner feelings. A skein dhu with a deer

Saucepans and kettles from the kitchen add weight and bulk to the backpacker, who only needs utensils for one person. Here our backpacker examines a typical cooking pot and a Meta 71 cup with lid. These are quite sufficient for most backpacking cooking.

Two pans on the Vango S 7300 speed up the delivery of food and hot drinks for small groups. Backpacking cooking pots are flat with broad bases for quick heating, and should be seamless and ridgeless for ease of cleaning. Good pans last — these are over 25 years old and are still going strong.

For a backpacker collecting kit from scratch the Trangia cooker is ideal, as it contains not only a stove but its own very high quality pans, and even a neat little 1-pint kettle. Pans are held by a pot-gripper, perforated to allow heat dispersal. Another lightweight pan with lid is the Optimus mess tin (5oz). The ubiquitous Meta 71 cup doubles as a mug for the ultimate in lightness.

hoof handle is one extreme, while at the other could be a Swiss Army knife with 27 gadgets all clustered between two pieces of red plastic. The need for a knife is actually low. Backpackers in Britain do not go out on hunting trips hoping to live off the land by trapping and snaring, so there is no need for a knife of the size and strength required to disembowel an animal and clean a hide.

The gadgeteering knife would come closest perhaps to practicality, with an efficient can opener, scissors, corkscrew, screwdriver, file and toothpick — if only the knife blade was big enough to make wooden tent pegs and fashion other things that get lost or broken along the trail.

Ideally the knife is just a knife, honed sharp and kept that way, housed efficiently either by folding or by sliding into a tough scabbard.

No fork is needed on the trail, but a dessert spoon will stir and measure, and carry food to the mouth. If made from stainless steel it will not discolour with use. Some packers take a small teaspoon as well, for added versatility.

Without gadgets on the knife, a tiny can opener can be tied to the pack with thread to stop getting lost, and is a useful addition, but only if eating out of cans is planned.

Drinking containers are another personal preference. Some like a pint mug made of plastic, some a stainless cup, and others prefer enamelware and are prepared to carry it.

In the United States, the backpacker's universal badge of office is a squat stainless steel drinking cup with a wire bale curved so that it can be worn under the belt. The Sierra Cup, as it is known, is not a very practical container. Its wide rim cools foods and drink far too rapidly, it is heavy for its size, and its narrow bottom lacks stability so it can be upset easily. Nevertheless, hundreds and thousands of Sierra Cups are sold every year.

Ideally, a drinking vessel for the backpacker should have at least a pint capacity — the working size of most soup mixes — and if lesser quantities are called for in packet sizes these can be accurately gauged from marks made on the inside of the vessel. It should have a good square wide bottom for stability when put down on uneven surfaces, it should not be hot on the tongue, and it should be easy to clean and light in weight. A pint plastic mug fits this bill fairly well.

There is no need for plates and bowls when backpacking — eating right from the pan is the aim. Water is often at a premium so washing up a string of dishes is undesirable. Mixing food ready for cooking is usually done right in the polybag which transports it and the bag can be properly disposed of on return from the trip.

A washkit is also fairly personal. The amount of washing done by backpackers is very variable ranging from a once-a-day sponge over with a damp cloth and wipe over the hands before bed to a full bath taken from a pint drinking mug. Trail dirt doesn't matter too much, and a sweat odour is acceptable to the man wearing it. Fancy deodorants have no place on the hike and neither do terry towelling bath robes. On the other hand, cellulose non-woven wiping cloths make ideal disposable hand and face cloths.

One method is to keep one cloth soaked in water and rubbed in soap in a polybag. This is used to wipe faces and fingers from time to time, and another dry one is used to clean up. Never in any circumstances take soap to running water — a spring, stream or river edge. Collect some water in a large polybag and carry it well away from the water's edge and wash more thoroughly there, disposing of the dirty water evenly over the ground. Of course a splash around in the sea or mountain stream is a great cleanser even without soap, and a couple of wipers soon dry off the skin.

There are bio-degradable soaps either in solid block or squeezy semi-liquid form. These work well even in sea water for the daily washover after breakfast. Generally speaking however, the attitude towards washing when backpacking should be that of a small boy who has a holy dread of soap and water.

Teeth cleaning can be done easily enough and there are special collapsible tooth brushes which weigh little and stow away in their own handles. Many packers of long standing use only salt for cleaning teeth.

Toilet paper is best carried in the form of paper handkerchieves. These handy packs make very good companions on the trail, not only for toilet paper, but as nose wipers, pot wipers, boot wipers and even fire lighters. Each pack should be stowed separately in a small polybag sealed up to prevent water damaging the contents.

A torch is necessary for emergency lighting and general use about camp. In summer months the size of the torch can be minimal — a small plastic job with two AA sized batteries and a prefocus bulb will suffice. Two deep saw cuts made in the plastic case at the end furthest away from the bulb will allow the flashlight to be held in the teeth while using both hands. A lanyard through a small hole drilled in the case helps too. A spare bulb should always be carried and manganese alkali batteries, although costing much more than Leclanche cells, last much longer at full power and recover better. Their shelf life is good, and so is their resistance to the effects of cold temperatures.

In winter packing, a much bigger flashlight or headlight is usually carried. Alternatively, thick stearine candles which will burn in still air for up to eight hours and give off a very good light, coupled with a small flashlight, are another way of passing the long hours of darkness in off-season packing.

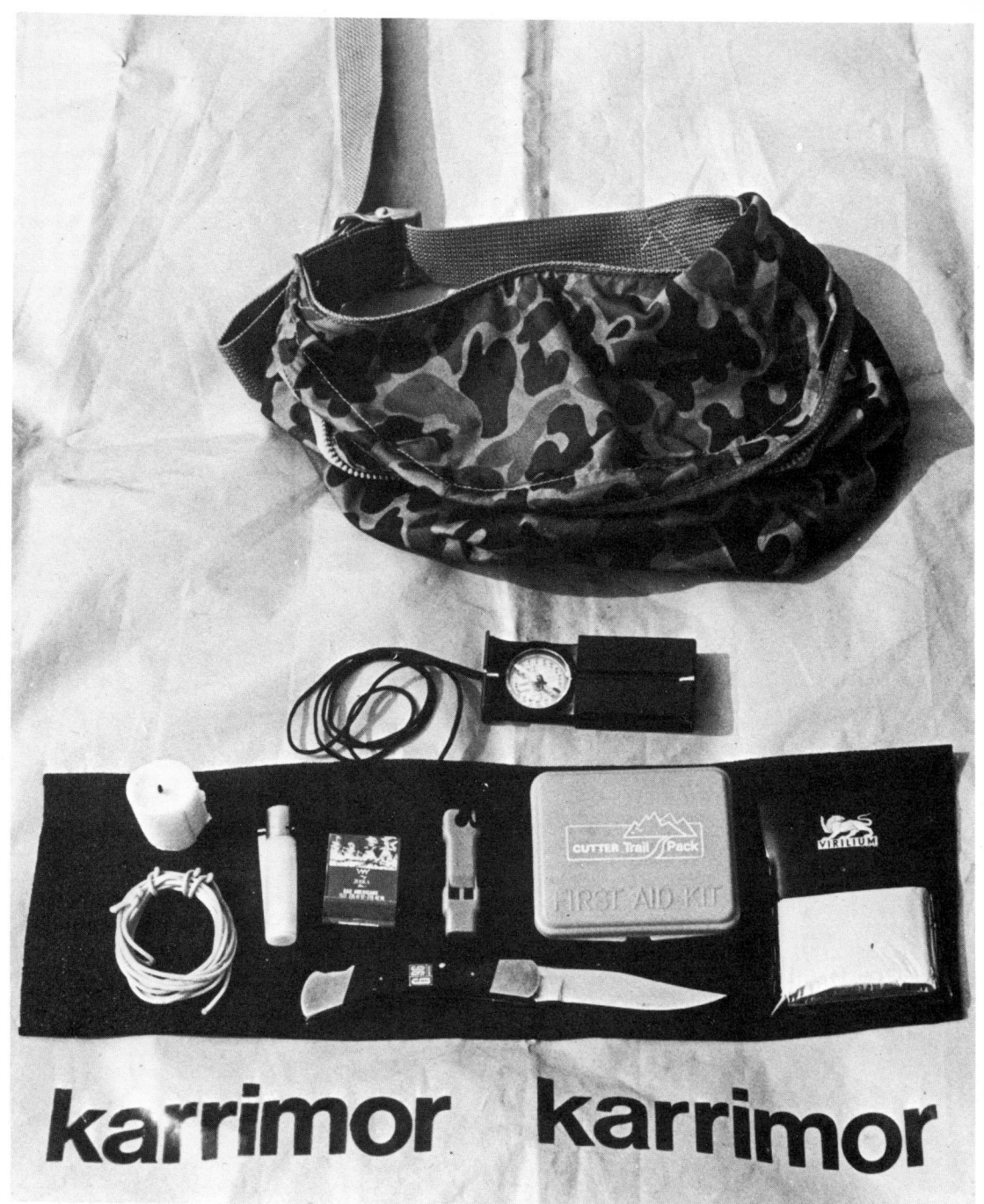

Hiking in hill country may face the backpacker with emergencies. On day hikes in mountains or moorland, where you can be caught out in fog, or a storm, it is advisable to carry an emergency kit such as that shown here. Carried in a Camp Trails waist pack, the weight will be unnoticed. This kit contains a compass, a whistle, candle stub, lighter and book of matches, piece of nylon cord, small first aid kit, a knife and a Virilium Heat sheet. (Total 1lb 8oz.) You could add a small bottle of water and some sort of emergency ration, such as chocolate or Turblokken. The waist pack will hold it all, and also a Karrimor Bivi bag or a cagoule.

Whistles are fun things to carry, especially when travelling in company, and can be used for communication over a wide distance. But other than calling distress signals in mountains, whistles have only a luxury value.

Compasses, providing they can be used, are much more necessary. These fine, but relatively cheap instruments, can orient a man in unfamiliar country, allow progress in mist over a known course, help the eye pick up cairns on otherwise featureless moorland and provide hours of fascination. Only liquid damped compasses should be used. Those mounted on clear plastic bases with scales and grid lines are of more use than hand bearing compasses worn on the wrist. No compass is worth carrying unless it can be used intelligently. It is even easier to get lost with a compass that cannot be read than following one's nose without.

A small first aid kit should be carried, but this will be dealt with in detail later on. Personal medicines, such as allergy relief, insulin and so on, should be carried in a small plastic wallet in a shirt pocket and not in the pack.

Maps are very necessary, but there is no point in carrying a whole map and its cover. It may be more convenient to slice out the section over which the hike is to be made, and to fold this into a waterproof cover made from a clear document case. Sections can be folded over and numbered for continuity to prevent "walking off the edge". Vague travel over a wide moorland area will need much more map than a defined trail measuring only yards across. Transfer the north point and grid references to the sections cut out of the main map.

Some of the major long distance footpaths have well mapped booklets written about them. These make better trail companions than maps — despite the extra weight of text.

Cameras, telescopes or binoculars, movie cameras and other bulky gear have a place in the pack of only those people willing to carry them. The serious backpacking photographer will not mind sacrificing some heavy kit to make room for his cameras and film, while the birdwatcher will not be parted from his 10 x 50s. A botanist is prepared to carry his field book and collecting box, and a meteorologist may need a miniature radio to hear the forecast, but in general, if a tyro backpacker is not yet a specialist, all such equipment merely adds to the load rather than the enjoyment. Of course, if one has the money, there is plenty of variety on the market in the way of really tiny cameras, radios, monoculars and such, but it is still extra clutter to carry.

Gear collected, there comes the main objective of backpacking which is hiking free where the fancy dictates.

Half the fun of backpacking is in planning a trip, whether it be a trial overnighter or a 14-day holiday in a remote corner of the country. Planning begins usually when the spirits are at their lowest ebb and the everyday world crowds in and makes life intolerable. Planning is part dreaming and part logistics. The dreaming projects images into the mind and makes it seethe with a desire to go to a certain corner of this beautiful island of ours. Good planning will turn that dream into reality and a memory to be cherished. Bad planning can turn a dream into a nightmare, and a disgust which makes a beginner give up backpacking forever.

The first overnight hike and camp teaches a newcomer more than any other similar period in his later career. It demonstrates that buying equipment is only part of the backpacking scene. Using it properly and discovering the shortcomings are much more important. With proper planning that first night can be the launch pad for memorable trips in later life.

Get down to basics for a moment. Will you be backpacking alone? In company of friends or the family? Or do you have a crony who has been packing before?

The loner is a rather special case. He accepts the loneliness as an esoteric pleasure he can only derive from packing. He accepts that everything he will need will have to be carried by himself alone — no sharing of communal equipment. He accepts the risks of being alone should be twist an ankle or break a leg in a lonely place. Going alone is not recommended for the first-timer. Lone packing needs a lot of courage and much experience.

Group packing is different. An item left at home can be tolerated in a group — provided it is not too vital, such as a sleeping bag. There are weight savings to be made from taking one cookset, one stove, one camera, one tent, one first aid pack, and so on. The ideal group parties are four in number — threesomes tend to break down into a twosome with one man left out.

Family packing is rather similar. Father gathers a natural fellowship from one child and mother one from another. Only the scale of the trip is reduced with a family — the pace is set by the youngest member and by the amount of equipment mother and father are prepared to carry for their children. Family packing can be a great deal of fun.

The man who has a crony who has been packing before starts with a big advantage. There will be a wealth of experience from which he can draw; a sober judgment of the amount of distance that can be covered; and a companionship which is hard to match in any other outdoor activity.

The planning of any trip is most essential, and especially that very first trip. There are lists to be made from which a master list for later trips can be built. There is food to be collected, divided up and stripped of useless, weighty packaging before being repacked into meal sized polybags. There is gear to be inspected very carefully for signs of weakness at

Backpacking is just as great for children as it is for adults. After a few trips in company with adults the children should be confident enough to try it on their own.

essential points. Harnesses on packs, grommets on tents, guy lines, stoves to check for leaks and proper working, fuel levels to be dipped; all these things need to be done.

Assuming that boots, socks and feet have now been properly mated and walked hard together for several miles, the first short trip close by one's home

can be made. The route will be familiar from close study of a good One Inch Popular series Ordnance Survey map, and likely overnight camping spots located — perhaps in advance — to make sure everything goes well on this first trip.

Then there remains nothing to do save packing, dressing, shouldering up and leaving.

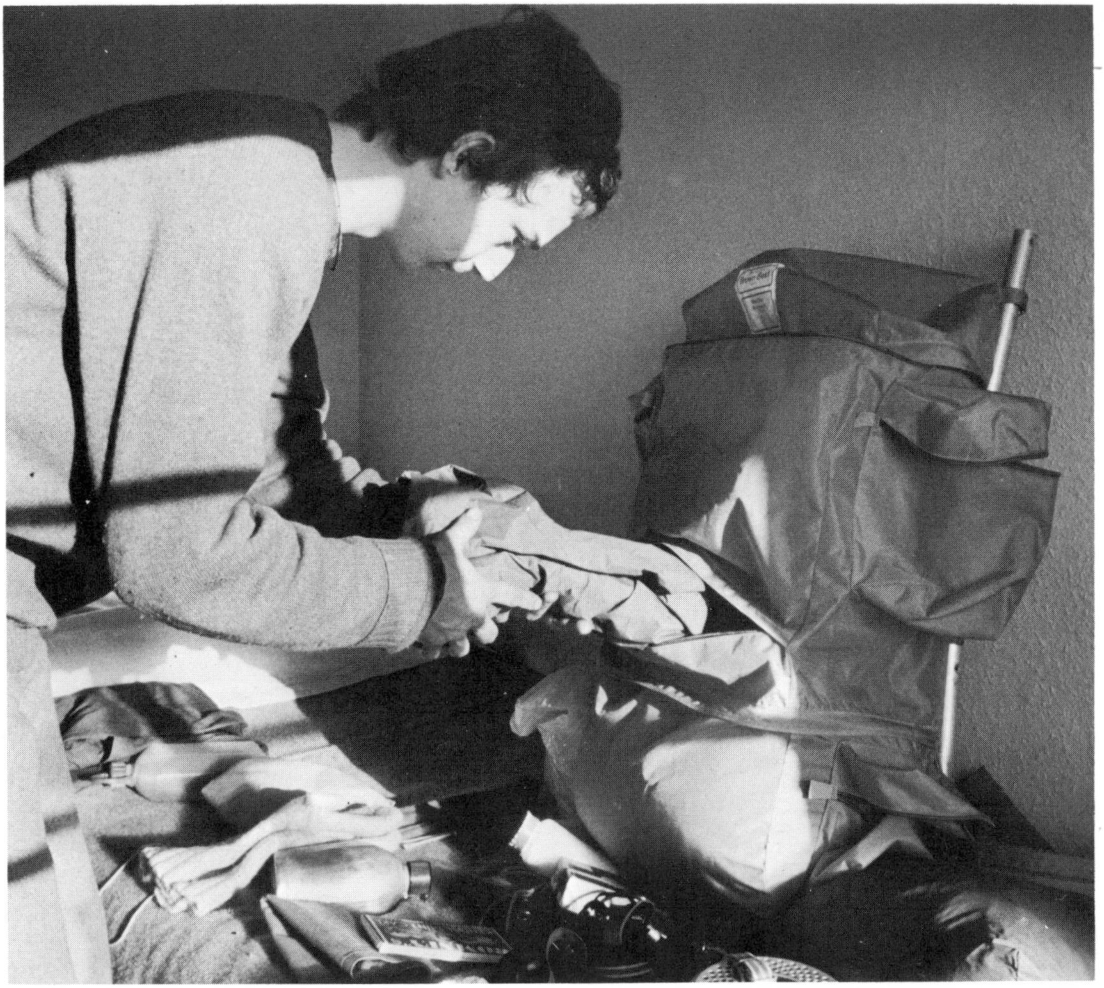

Packing up is done carefully, and according to individual check lists.

The journey begins once the backpacker closes his front door. Public transport will take the hiker to almost every area of Britain.

a day on the trail

The Peak Forest, north of Tideswell, is stone wall country, close to the start of the Pennine Way.

A walking-stick is of great help in this sort of situation. Wet boulders are slippery and dangerous and this hiker in Wharfedale needs all the support he can get.

On the open moors, near Skipton in Yorkshire. Climbing in tussocky grass calls for a shortened step and sure footing. A nylon cagoule keeps out the wind.

Hiking is not just walking. Hiking with a pack is using every ounce of energy to good advantage. The stride will settle down to a proper length after the first mile or so, and if a conscious effort is made to make a little kick with each forward swing of the leg there will be a sense of gain and some extra footage for each mile. The whole body will learn to swing, trunk and shoulders turning slightly on the hips as the weight of the pack moves forward. Arms are swung actively if not vigorously in a diagonal movement and, properly timed with each stride, will add balance and drive to the gait.

When the trail starts to climb it is best to shorten the stride and still keep the same pace. Never take long laborious strides with a pack. Inch by inch at the same pace as before is the message. Breathing is also important, and as the angle increases the number of breaths per stride is a conscious action.

Going downhill is not as easy as it sounds. The knees should be slightly bent and the stance upright. If a slip comes the leg can be bent further to maintain balance without loss of composure. A full slide should be countered by turning to the side and then to face the slide. Never glissade with a pack, for it can become uncontrollable.

Many experienced backpackers have a walking staff to give them a third leg, and this is good advice. When boulder hopping in a river bed the staff can determine which stone is secure even before a stride is made. With a strong current the staff becomes a great safety feature. A staff can also replace a tent pole and thereby save pack weight, but ensure the tip has an orthopaedic rubber cap which easily deforms to any surface to give a proper grip.

Dressing is most important but it is very often overlooked. The idea is to walk cool. To sweat is to

Regular rests are advisable. A tired backpacker loses some of the enjoyment of the trip. Here a hiker relaxes beside the Brecon Canal.

waste energy. So although a packer starts off fairly well clothed he is soon stripping and opening shirt fronts to vent as soon as the work produces heat. Only when the wind is facing a packer does he close up. The method of clothing up described earlier will give the handiest regulation of heat balance when hiking hard with a pack. But there is always a hotspot behind the shoulder blades and under the pack. This must be protected when the first halt is called and the pack sloughed off. A windproof jacket is then put on to prevent sudden chills.

Eyes are always the packer's most important equipment. He must be keeping a close look at the trail under his feet, conning ahead to see that he is not running into a blind alley or onto a sand spit with no relief. It is best to stop a second when doing a grand scan of the horizon. That way the footing is secure and the detail is not missed.

Resting is a matter of personal preference which develops as the art of backpacking is learned, but as a general guide, a rest stop every hour for five minutes is recommended. This entails no more than slipping out of the pack, adjusting the laces or inspecting a warm spot on the foot, a bite of trail food, a wipe of the brow and off again. More than five minutes induces lethargy.

A lunch stop is more lengthy. The insulating foam pad is removed from the pack and spread out, and a billy of water set on the stove for soup or tea. Boots are off and socks spread out to air, and tied to the pack if soaked with sweat to be substituted by a fresh pair. If there is rain and no shelter, the fly of the tent should be erected. Shelter comes first to a backpacker no matter what his other needs.

Hiking goes on all afternoon until the sun angle is about 20 degrees. Then a site must be found, which, with proper planning should be reasonably near to hand anyway.

Halts should not be too long, or it becomes hard to get into one's stride again. A walker gets away again after a tea break beside Chanctonbury Ring on the South Downs Way.

Lunch stops are an opportunity to brew up soup or a hot drink and to plan the rest of the day. In Wales, on the Offa's Dyke Path, the scenery can be enjoyed over a leisurely cup of tea.

Below
Trail snacks fill in the gaps between meals. Backpackers should follow this lamb's example and eat when feeling tired or hungry. Trail food includes chocolate, biscuits, peanuts, raisins and compressed fruit bars.

Like the sheep, keep moving after a meal until it is time to look for water and a site for the night stop.

Provided that purifying tablets are carried, water points can be found fairly easily in most parts of the British countryside. Avoid totally stagnant water though.

Above
If no better protection can be found, pitch the tent, tail into wind, on the flattest piece of ground available.
Right
In stone wall country, a pitch close to the wall will break the force of the wind and will help to ensure a quieter night's sleep.

Sites are never ideal but there are some basic requirements. A flat site is best, but a slightly sloping site should be head high. A lush meadow at the foot of high ground should not be chosen, because night drainage of cool air will chill the site perhaps as much as ten degrees below that of ground maybe only thirty feet higher up. A hedge, stone wall, ditch side, bank, or rock outcrop on the weather side is an experienced backpacker's first site requirement. He knows the protection it will afford him during the night. Water used to be high on the list of needs, but with modern packing this has been demoted — a night's supply is carried the last few miles of the afternoon. Before setting up the tent the ground is covered on hands and knees with much thoroughness. A pine cone, stone or mole hill can ruin a good night's sleep. Then with shelter from a nearby low hedge or wall — never under trees, especially deciduous trees — the tent is set up tail to wind.

Above
Moorland country frequently provides ideal camp sites like this one. Clean water is on hand, and there is level pitching for the tents. Providing there is no mist, this site will be dry and sheltered from the wind.

Right
Generally speaking though, a site at the bottom of a valley such as this will attract mist and lower temperatures at night. Both lead to heavy condensation in nylon tents.

Above far right
Pitching on the side of a hill gives a better view over the surrounding countryside, and the rising sun will dry the tents earlier.

Below far right
While the bottom of the valley is still shrouded in mist, these backpackers are packing up while sleeping bags air and flysheets dry out in the early morning sun.

The insulating pad is slipped under the tent ground cloth to prevent any sharp projection penetrating the material and also to stop the pad moving around under a sleeping body.

The sleeping bag is then removed from the stuff sack, shaken out and the head end folded over to prevent any insect creeping inside. At intervals before bedtime the bag is shaken over again to gain its full loft by the time it is needed.

With pack off, a billy of water is set on the stove for a leisurely cup of tea or coffee, and supper is prepared. This is now a simple meal with the minimum of cooking. Any dried fruit which needs soaking for morning can be set aside in warm water and covered over. A final sponge over, a gentle stroll around camp, and then to bed.

Never sleep in trail clothes, but have them handy stowed in a large polybag in case of emergency or if the night turns very cold. It is best to sleep with as near nothing on as possible, sure in the knowledge that there is more warmth available if necessary — remember thickness is warmth!

Some packers keep a little diary of their daily achievements. This is also a convenient way of remembering the things not to do next time. Some make a tiny mark on the map at each rest stop to check on progress. Some go backpacking not for itself alone but to watch birds, or to find new specimens of botany or insects. Whatever the reason, the last few moments before bed are best; they are tired, happy from their achievements, and

The insulating mat is unrolled and put under the groundsheet of the tent.

Then the sleeping bag is taken out of its stuff sack and given a thorough shaking to fluff up the down before the bag is laid out in the tent.

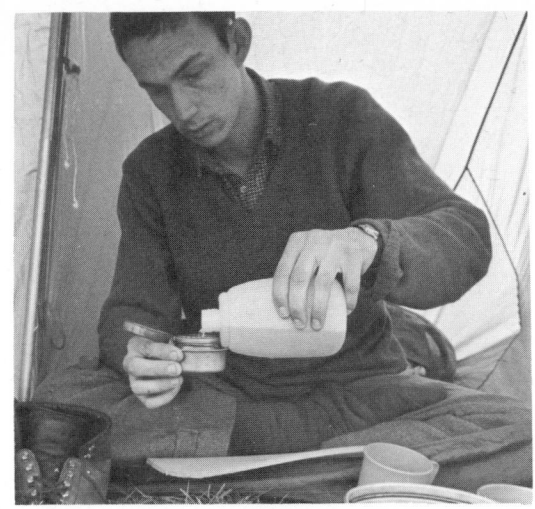

sure in the knowledge that they have accepted a challenge and done much more than they expected — certainly more than their pre-backpacking friends would do.

The night's rest is the most important sector of the day's activities. A full eight or even nine hours should be spent in the sleeping bag. At first — especially on that first night out — deep sleep will come straight away. Then after about a couple of hours comes wakefulness. This is normal. The edge of fatigue has been dulled, the bed is strange, the sheer unfamiliarity is novel and animal senses are aroused. After a little while though, slumber returns and before one knows it the glow of dawn warms the eastern side of the canopy of the tent.

Boots should have been opened fully the night before and drawn inside the tent to air thoroughly. This is a good place to stow a small torch in case of need in the night.

As the evening draws on, the stove is lit and the evening meal cooked and eaten.

In winter, a thick stearine candle provides heat as well as light, and warms up a small tent quickly.

The end of the day.

Then as the light gets stronger and detail can be seen, a pan of water set out the night before should be put to boil for that early morning cuppa. All this can be, and should be done from inside the sleeping bag. Even the dried fruit can be eaten in bed without dribbling sticky fluid onto the sleeping bag.

By now the light is strong and the sun just about to peep over the horizon and here is another lesson the tyro soon learns — noting the position of the sun from the previous morning to ensure his tent catches that first light and is not shut in by hills.

The sleeping bag can be put to air outside on good mornings just as soon as the dew is dried off the fly sheet. On bad mornings one must do one's best. Always stuff the bag into its sack last thing before striking camp.

Breakfast, much along the lines described earlier, a wash, a restow of the pack, and then off again — perhaps before six thirty — certainly before seven. Those early hours on the trail are the best in the whole hiking day.

Right
If everything is put near at hand the night before, breakfast can be eaten and a cup of tea brewed and drunk without getting out of bed.

Below
After breakfast, pack up carefully and ensure nothing is left behind.

Of course backpacking is not all sunshine and scented pine forest.

Rain, fog, wind, snow even, and all the combinations nature can devise are likely to come the backpacker's way. At first, on short trips into nearby country, a little rain doesn't matter too much. This sort of exposure to the elements is good training for developing the stoicism necessary in the good backpacker. He knows he is well equipped, and as he increases his knowledge his ability to move freely around the countryside without caring a fig for the weather is all part of the game. Nor is it roughing it. Only tenderfoots rough it.

There are but two main hazards that a newcomer must get to recognise early and learn how to deal with: sunshine and exposure.

Getting sunburnt is just plain stupidity. Keep covered. Wear a light hat in high summer. A sun-burned skin is extremely painful and can threaten safety. A little lip salve carried in the first aid pack is a good idea.

Speaking of the first aid pack, nothing elaborate is implied. Just a few codeine tablets in a foil covering, a couple of adhesive bandages, some Dr Scholl's moleskin for blisters, a stick of lip salve, some water purification tablets to dose doubtful water, a few safety pins, a needle with thread, and that is about it. Personal medication is needed of course. The whole lot can be folded into a stiff polybag and sealed with adhesive tape.

Above
Part of the fun of backpacking lies in the sights of the trail itself, not just reaching the end. This statue of St Christopher crafted from small billets of wood stands 100 yards from the South Downs Way. Backpackers learn to keep their eyes open for the unusual.

Below
Open country in summer can give an incautious packer a bad case of wind and sunburn. You can even suffer from exposure. Carry some sunburn cream, and a hat, for protection against sun. Carry the right clothing and shelter for protection against exposure.

Conditions in the mountains can change rapidly. While this hiker stopped for lunch, a hail storm hit the area. Within seconds, the hills 'whited out' and the temperature fell ten degrees.

Exposure is much more serious than sunburn. It can strike even in summer at lower altitudes. It comes about when the hardworked body is short of energy and the blood can no longer supply limbs and vital organs with enrichment. If the wind is blowing, and clothes are damp from too much sweating or rain perhaps, you must be especially on guard against the exposure danger.

Only the experienced can read the warning symptoms in others, and the inexperienced find it difficult to read them in themselves.

Here are some symptoms to be remembered:

Giddiness, affected vision, uncontrollable laughter and unaccountable bursts of activity, slurred speech, shivering, anger, a desire to quit. One or several symptoms may be present.

The first action must be to stop, set up a tent, shake out a sleeping bag, roll out insulating mat, make a warm sweet drink, strip off wet clothing and replace with dry and then get inside the bag done right up at the head until the shivering stops and equilibrium is obtained. Further warm sweet drinks should be made and some more solid food of a cereal base laced with glucose should follow. STAY IN THE SLEEPING BAG FOR SOME LITTLE TIME.

Foggy days on high ground, windy days with no sun, heavy sweating on windy days, heavy rain that soaks clothing, rapidly falling temperatures on an empty stomach towards the end of the day are all danger periods. Remedial action must be taken immediately — every minute counts to restore equilibrium. To delay can spell death. For rapid shelter in case of real emergency, carry a heat sheet or spare blanket.

A backpacker's First Aid kit should contain, at least, some plaster strips of varying lengths and widths, gauze dressings, antiseptic cream, aspirin and painkiller tablets, anti-allergy ointment and water-purification pills. Also in the kit should be a needle and thread, safety pins, razor blade and some "Moleskin" for boot-worn feet.

For the rest, backpacking is common sense. The good packer never tries to do too much. He is deliberate in his movements. He doesn't jump down or try to climb over high walls with a pack on. He is reasonably sanitary in his habits. He rests well whenever he can. He never runs around bare footed and always attends to a warm spot developing on his feet. He never takes shortcuts he is unsure of. He tells people at home where he is going and when he intends to get back. He never packs with a cold or recovering from some mild illness. He always gets in some practice walking before leaving on a longer trip. He is forever stripping weight from his pack — most important this.

At the end of each trip he tips out all his kit and makes three piles of the stuff; one containing all the stuff he never used, the stuff he used once and the stuff he used regularly.

The pile of gear that never got used should contain his first aid pack, but most of the rest can be discarded for the next trip. Scrutiny of the second pile should reveal stuff that can be eliminated or combined with other equipment. In that way, together with his diary of notes made on the trail, his master check list gets compiled.

After examination, all gear gets cleaned, repaired and stowed away properly for the next trip. Tents can be set up and completely aired in the garden before stowing properly. Sleeping bags can be pulled from the stuff sack and loosely folded in the airing cupboard. Mud and dirt can be cleaned from boots and perhaps given a light coating of dubbing. Poly bottles are washed out and left in the pantry with the lids off. Fine wool socks are washed gently in tepid water with Stergene, and the same with wool shirts. Mud is washed off waterproofs and gaiters. Stoves are cleaned and refilled. All is then ready for that next trip that the newcomer will join with the experienced and be forever dreaming about until the first footing is made.

Britain is bursting with beautiful places to pack into. This lovely woodland path is in the Forest of Dean, near Symonds Yat in Gloucestershire.

Offa's Dyke Path crosses part of the Black Mountains which offer the walker solitude among sheep and ponies on long, high, heather-covered ridges, and in sheltered green valleys below.

Most people think first of the mountains, but this wild, majestic country of Scotland, Wales and the North of England is not for the novice on the first trip. It is better to start in more friendly country, on the open moors or the Downs, along the coast or the canals, until one is more used to backpacking habits. Hardly anywhere in England is not crossed by a footpath, and it is possible to walk, explore and camp within a few miles of most peoples' home areas.

For solitude, the hills and highlands of Scotland are magnetic for many. The walking is mainly over heather moors, with views to the sea and the lochs, while for the hardier souls there is the allure of a climb to the top of one of the loftier bens. Bear in mind though that the risk of mist, fog, wind and exposure increase in such lonely, largely treeless localities, so the need for telling someone your intended route is greater than if you are planning to visit some more populated place.

The chalk Downs of Southern England offer a peace of their own, entirely different to that of real mountains, but just as refreshing to the jaded soul. Despite the onslaught of modern development, there are still places along the Berkshire Ridgeway where in imagination one can see the movement of migrant British tribes between the barrows and the ancient hill forts.

For quiet days in summer, hiking the length of a canal brings a varied tapestry of countryside to the backpacker. The towpaths are flat and make for easy walking, while the number of pubs by the locks and along the banks provide good catering and many excuses for stopping for refreshment in the sun. Canals traverse some amazing obstacles, following the contours round hills and crossing valleys on viaducts.

The coastal paths are best enjoyed in the off-season periods unless one hankers for the

The Berkshire Ridgeway is one of the oldest tracks in Britain. Along this section of the Lambourn Downs you will pass Iron Age forts and the barrows of long-dead British chiefs, and will come eventually to the great stone circle at Avebury.

A walker nears the Petersfield end of the South Downs Way near Buriton. This view is to the North, to the Alton ridge.

The Monmouthshire and Brecon Canal, near Abergavenny in South Wales, winds through hill country above the valley of the River Usk.

The Forest of Dean, near Christchurch in Gloucestershire, once supplied timber for Britain's ships. Coal is still mined in the forest which is now controlled by the Forestry Commission. Not far away, a short section of original Roman road has been uncovered.

The beaches of the East Coast are mostly shingle, and the walking is easiest near the water. In all seasons of the year, the wind off the sea adds a chill factor to the exposure risk. The backpacker needs warm clothing, and good shelter with a secure method of pegging into sand.

Wild ponies may be found on open moorland in many parts of Britain, such as Dartmoor, Exmoor and the Welsh hills. These ones are on a ridge in the Black Mountains near Hay-on-Wye.

company of other holidaymakers. Something about the sea, and the cliffs and rocks and shoreline, has always fascinated the British, and hiking in areas such as Cornwall, Essex or Northumberland gives rich rewards to the backpacker. The longest footpath in the country is the South West Peninsula Path, 515 miles round the coast of Dorset, Devon and Cornwall.

Other long-distance footpaths include the Pennine Way up the spine of England (in high season, the backpacking equivalent of a motorway), the Offa's Dyke Path which traverses Wales and the southern Marches in a North-South line, the North Downs Way, the South Downs Way, the Berkshire Ridgeway and the Pembrokeshire Coast Path. Other areas of outstanding natural beauty include the Lake District, the North Yorkshire Moors, the Yorkshire Dales, the Peak District of Derbyshire, Snowdonia in North Wales, the Black Mountains and the Brecon Beacons in South Wales, the Suffolk Coast, the New Forest, and Exmoor and Dartmoor in the West. Hadrian's Wall, the Dark Peak, Breckland, the Forest of Dean, the Mendips, the Cotswolds, the Chilterns . . . the catalogue is endless, and there is something for everyone.

All these have their own special attractions and provide different types of hiking, calling for minor variations in the equipment used. For example, the South Downs combine much open country with old and new forestry, and the trail is always flint and chalk. This makes for very hard walking calling for a thicker and stiffer sole than that used for walking a peat moor. Again, better tentage is needed when planning to camp in the windswept uplands of North Yorkshire than when down in a wooded area such as the New Forest, where the trees give shelter from wind.

Wharfedale is in the Yorkshire Dales National Park. From Barden Fell, this picture shows the view to the North West towards Grassington, with Appletreewick in the right foreground.

The little lake called 'Llyn-cwm-Llwch' makes a good resting place for a couple who have walked down from Corn Du (2863ft), the peak in the background. Pen y fan (2907 feet), the highest point in the Brecon Beacons, is half a mile to the left of Corn Du.

Follow the Country Code at all times when you are backpacking. Close all gates; farm animals are valuable, and an open gate allows them to stray.

Finally, some points to remember:

All land in Britain is owned by someone, either the Crown, a local Corporation or a private individual or concern. Always ask for permission to camp before pitching on a chosen site as it saves the embarrassment of being told to move.

It will do no harm to remind the reader again that even in summer when the weather in Britain is generally at its best and warmest, some form of cold weather clothing and protection should be carried when backpacking in the open hills, in case of sudden changes in conditions. Rainwear, gloves and a balaclava hat will help to ensure that the backpacker is always comfortable and safe in any weather, so as to avoid becoming a burden and a liability to others.

Follow the Country Code at all times, and leave no trace of your passing. Litter is a real problem all over the world. Backpackers can help keep Britain that little bit greener if they make a point of packing out not only their own rubbish but a bit more besides. It is a good feeling to leave a beautiful place looking cleaner than it was when you first saw it. It is said in America that a backpacker should "Leave nothing but footprints, take nothing but photographs". One might add to this, "Leave behind your thanks, and take away your litter".

Backpacking, practised well and applied as an artform, brings all these fabulous places of Britain to the foot. They are there to be enjoyed in whatever mood one approaches them, and as the seasons change, so they change too. Backpacking in Britain beckons. Enjoy it now.

Just about anywhere in Britain can be reached by a footpath. The choice is yours.

This map shows the best known National Parks and long distance footpaths in England and Wales.

National Parks in England and Wales

Lake District	866 sq. miles
Snowdonia	845 sq. miles
Yorkshire Dales	680 sq. miles
North Yorkshire Moors	553 sq. miles
Peak District	542 sq. miles
Brecon Beacons	519 sq. miles
Northumberland	398 sq. miles
Dartmoor	365 sq. miles
Exmoor	365 sq. miles
Pembrokeshire Coast	224 sq. miles

Long-distance footpaths

Pennine Way	250 miles
Offa's Dyke Path	168 miles
Pembrokeshire Coast Path	167 miles
North Downs Way	141 miles
North Cornwall Coast Path	134 miles
South Cornwall Coast Path	133 miles
Cleveland Way	93 miles
South Devon Coast Path	92 miles
Ridgeway Path	85 miles
Somerset and North Devon Coast Path	82 miles
South Downs Way	80 miles
Dorset Coast Path	72 miles
Cotswold Way	100 miles

Country Code

Guard against all risk of fire — Plantations, woodlands and heaths are highly inflammable: every year acres burn because of casually dropped matches, cigarette ends or pipe ash.

Fasten all gates — even if you found them open. Animals can't be told to stay where they're put. A gate left open invites them to wander, a danger to themselves, to crops, and to traffic.

Keep dogs under proper control — Farmers have good reason to regard visiting dogs as pests; in the country a civilised town dog can become a savage. Keep your dog on a lead wherever there is livestock about, also on country roads.

Keep to the paths across farm land — Crops can be ruined by people's feet. Remember that grass is a valuable crop too, sometimes the only one on the farm. Flattened corn or hay is very difficult to harvest.

Avoid damaging fences, hedges and walls — They are expensive items in the farm's economy; repairs are costly and use scarce labour. Keep to recognised routes, using gates and stiles.

Leave no litter — All litter is unsightly, and some is dangerous as well. Take litter home for disposal; in the country it costs a lot to collect it.

Safeguard water supplies — Your chosen walk may well cross a catchment area for the water supply of millions. Avoid polluting it in any way. Never interfere with cattle troughs.

Protect wild life, wild plants and trees — Wild life is best observed, not collected. To pick or uproot flowers, carve trees and rocks, or disturb wild animals and birds, destroys other people's pleasure as well.

Go carefully on country roads — Country roads have special dangers: blind corners, high banks and hedges, slow-moving tractors and farm machinery or animals. Motorists should reduce their speed and take extra care; walkers should keep to the right, facing oncoming traffic.

Respect the life of the countryside — Set a good example and try to fit in with the life and work of the countryside. This way good relations are preserved, and those who follow are not regarded as enemies.

A possible starter kit for summer backpacking — minimum kit at minimum weight. This can be expanded later on to be an all-seasons kit, as all the equipment shown is top grade in its class.

		lbs.	ozs.
1.	Brown Best Super Ariel rucksack.	1	02
2.	Point Five Nimbus sleeping bag.	2	12
3.	1-gallon folding plastic water bottle.		04
4.	56" Karrimat.		10
5.	Optimus cooking pan with lid.		05
6.	Vango S 7000 butane gas stove with cartridge.		08
7.	1-pint plastic mug.		02
8.	Meta-71 boiling cup with lid.		02
9.	Spoon.		01
10.	Waterproof (this one is the Saunders Pakjak)		11
11.	Karrimor Bivi bag (Shelter).	1	00
12.	Pocket knife.		02
		7	11

Add food, water and personal clothing.

A possible comprehensive summer kit: although not everything is needed for every trip, this list will cover most of the options for summer packing.

		lbs.	ozs.
1.	56" Karrimat.		10
2.	Karrimor Marathon Tent.	2	04
3.	Showerproof hat.		02
4.	Mountain Equipment 'Lightline' sleeping bag.	1	15
5.	Poles and pegs for Marathon tent.	1	00
6.	Spare pair of loopstitch socks.		04
7.	Brown Best Pakkabed airbed.	1	11
8.	Helly-Hansen Polar Suit (acts as night wear and spare clothing)	1	15
9.	Sigg metal water bottles.		06
10.	Vango S 7000 butane gas stove and fuel canister.		14
11.	Mountain Equipment's Down sweater.	1	00
X1	Green Top polybottles.		02
X2.	Foot powder.		01
12.a	Robert Saunders' Pakjak poncho.		11
12.b	Henri-Lloyd Orkney overtrousers.		07
13.	Dachstein mitts.		05
14.	Maps.		04 each
15.	Optimus cooking pot with lid.		05
16.	Robert Lawrie XXXI R boots with Vibram sole.	3	12
17.	Meta-71 boiling cup with lid.		02
18.	J-cloth in plastic bag.		02
19.	Spoon.		01
20.	Folding pocket knife.		05
21.	Washing kit.		04
22.	Matches in waterproof tin with screwtop lid.		01
23.	Torch.		03
24.	Nylon string.		—
25.	Compass and whistle.		03
26.	Book matches and candle stub.		02
27.	Map measurer.		—
28.	Tin opener.		02
29.	Lip salve.		—
30.	Comb.		—
31.	Brown Best "Super Ariel" rucksack.	1	02
32.	Virilium Heat Sheet.		01
33.	Belt pack.		08
34.	Paper handkerchieves.		—
35.	First aid kit.		04
		21	08

A possible comprehensive winter kit.

	lbs.	ozs.
1. 78" Karrimat insulating mat.	1	02
2. Woollen Balaclava helmet.		03
3. Mountain Equipment's Snowline sleeping bag.	2	15
4. Robert Saunders' Lite Hike tent with "Extreme" flysheet.	3	00
5. Poles and pegs for Lite Hike tent.	1	00
6. Spare pair of loopstitch socks.		04
7. Brown Best Pakkabed airbed.	1	11
8. Helly-Hansen Polar suit.	1	15
9. Sigg metal water bottles, empty.		06
10. Sigg fuel bottle, empty.		03
11. SVEA 123 petrol stove, with boiling cup lid.	1 -	02
12. Pouring spout lid for Sigg fuel bottle.		01
13/14. Green Top polybottles.		02
15. Footpowder.		—
16. Mountain Equipment "Cerro Torre" Dacron Duvet.	1	15
17. MOAC oilcloth waterproof parka.	1	06
18. Helly-Hansen nylon pile mitts.		05
19. Henri-Lloyd Orkney overtrousers.		07
20. Robert Lawrie XXX1 R boots with Vibram soles.	3	12
21. Maps.		04 each
22. Two 1½ pint cooking pots, and 1 pint plastic mug.		09
23. J-cloth in plastic bag.		—
24. Spoon.		01
25. Folding pocket knife.		05
26. Pot lifter for cooking pots.		07
27. Washing kit.		04
28. Matches in waterproof tin with screw top.		01
29. Torch.		03
30. Map measurer, tin opener and lip salve.		02
31. Nylon string.		—
32. Compass and whistle.		03
33. Book matches and candle stub.		02
34. Comb.		—
35. Toilet paper in plastic bag.		—
36. Camp Trails Ponderosa pack on 515 Astral Pack frame.	4	00
37. Virilium Heat Sheet.		01
38. First Aid kit.		04
39. Paper handkerchieves.		—
40. Stuff sack for Karrimat, duvet etc.		05
	28	10

Add food, water, fuel and spare clothing as necessary.

This is NOT all pack weight — some of this is clothing and boot weight. The fact remains that when you backpack in cold, wet winter conditions, you will probably be carrying upwards of 30lbs on your back.

ADDRESSES OF MANUFACTURERS

Karrimor Weathertite Products Ltd: 19 Avenue Parade, Accrington, Lancs
Tents, frames, packs, stoves.

Brown Best and Company Ltd: 47 Old Woolwich Road, London SE10 9PU
Frames, sacks, airbed.

Camp Trails International Inc: Waterford Industrial Estate, Waterford, Ireland
Packframes, sacks.

Point Five
Banton and Co. Ltd: Meadow Lane, Nottingham NG2 3HP
Tents, sleeping bags, stoves, packs, frames.

Mountain Equipment
George Street, Glossop, Derbyshire SK13 8AY
Sleeping bags, duvets and cold weather clothing.

Mountaineering Activities Ltd: Wellington Place, Liverpool Road, Manchester, M3 4NQ.
Tents, boots, raingear, climbing equipment.

Helly Hansen (UK) Ltd: Ronald Close, Kempston, Bedford.
Warm clothing, raingear.

Henri Lloyd: 390 Manchester Road East, Worsley, Manchester, M28 6WR.
Raingear.

Vango (Scotland) Ltd: 356 Amulree Street, Glasgow G32 7SL.
Stoves, tents, sleeping bags, boots, raingear.

Robert Saunders and Co: Five Oaks Lane, Chigwell, Essex.
Tents, ponchos.

John Hawley and Co. Ltd: Goodall Works, Bloxwich Road, Walsall WS3 2UZ.
Tents.

Ultimate Equipment Ltd: The Butts, Warkworth, Morpeth, Northumberland.
Tents, outdoor clothing, climbing helmets.

Berghaus: 34 Dean Street, Newcastle upon Tyne, NE1 1PG.
Packs, boots.

AB Optimus Ltd. — CEGB Depot: Kempton, Hardwick, Bedford.
Stoves.

Suppliers

YHA Services, 29 John Adam Street, London WC2N 6JE
Also: 36—38 Fountain Street, Manchester M2 2BE
   35 Cannon Street, Birmingham B2 5EE

Pindisports: 14 Holborn, London EC1N 7LJ

Black's of Greenock: Ruxley Corner, Sidcup, Kent DA14 5AQ.

Ellis Brigham: 6/14 Cathedral Street, Manchester M4 3FU
Also: 73 Bold St., Liverpool 1.
   Market Jew St., Penzance, Cornwall.
   162 Whiteladies Rd., Bristol.

Field and Trek (Equipment) Ltd: 25 Kings Road, Brentwood, Essex.

The Practical Camper: (Mike Mariott and George Raven), 24 Market Street, Sandwich, Kent.

Graham Tiso: 44 Rodney Street, Edinburgh 7.

Alpine Sports Ltd: 309/311 Brompton Road, London SW3.

Alpine Sports Ltd: 138 Western Road, Brighton.

Other Useful Addresses

The Countryside Commission: 1 Cambridge Gate, London NW1.
Brochures and details of the National Parks and long-distance footpaths.

The Countryside Commission (Scotland): Battleby, Redgorton, Perth, Scotland.
Information for Scotland, as above.

British Tourist Authority: 64 St. James, London SW1.

Northern Ireland Tourist Board: 10 Royal Avenue, Belfast, 1, Northern Ireland.

Scottish Tourist Board: 2 Rutland Place, West End, Edinburgh, 1.

Wales Tourist Board: 3 Castle Street, Cardiff.

Youth Hostels Association: Trevelyan House, 8 St. Stephen's Hill, St. Albans, Herts.

Ramblers' Association: 1—4 Crawford Mews, York Street, London W1H 1PT.

Backpackers Club: Eric Gurney, National Organiser, 20 St. Michael's Road, Tilehurst, Reading.